An Analysis of

Augustine's

Confessions

Jonathan D. Teubner

LONDON AND NEW YORK

Published by Macat International Ltd
24:13 Coda Centre, 189 Munster Road, London SW6 6AW.

Distributed exclusively by Routledge
2 Park Square, Milton Park, Abingdon, Oxon OX14 4RN
605 Third Avenue, New York, NY 10017

Routledge is an imprint of the Taylor & Francis Group, an informa business

www.macat.com
info@macat.com

Cataloguing in Publication Data
A catalogue record for this book is available from the British Library.
Library of Congress Cataloguing-in-Publication Data is available upon request.
Cover illustration: Capucine Deslouis

ISBN 978-1-912303-83-0 (hardback)
ISBN 978-1-912127-98-6 (paperback)
ISBN 978-1-912282-71-5 (e-book)

Notice
The information in this book is designed to orientate readers of the work under analysis,
to elucidate and contextualise its key ideas and themes, and to aid in the development
of critical thinking skills. It is not meant to be used, nor should it be used, as a
substitute for original thinking or in place of original writing or research. References and
notes are provided for informational purposes and their presence does not constitute
endorsement of the information or opinions therein. This book is presented solely for
educational purposes. It is sold on the understanding that the publisher is not engaged
to provide any scholarly advice. The publisher has made every effort to ensure that
this book is accurate and up-to-date, but makes no warranties or representations with
regard to the completeness or reliability of the information it contains. The information
and the opinions provided herein are not guaranteed or warranted to produce particular
results and may not be suitable for students of every ability. The publisher shall not be
liable for any loss, damage or disruption arising from any errors or omissions, or from
the use of this book, including, but not limited to, special, incidental, consequential or
other damages caused, or alleged to have been caused, directly or indirectly, by the
information contained within.

CONTENTS

THE MACAT LIBRARY

The Macat Library is a series of unique academic explorations of seminal works in the humanities and social sciences – books and papers that have had a significant and widely recognised impact on their disciplines. It has been created to serve as much more than just a summary of what lies between the covers of a great book. It illuminates and explores the influences on, ideas of, and impact of that book. Our goal is to offer a learning resource that encourages critical thinking and fosters a better, deeper understanding of important ideas.

Each publication is divided into three Sections: Influences, Ideas, and Impact. Each Section has four Modules. These explore every important facet of the work, and the responses to it.

This Section-Module structure makes a Macat Library book easy to use, but it has another important feature. Because each Macat book is written to the same format, it is possible (and encouraged!) to cross-reference multiple Macat books along the same lines of inquiry or research. This allows the reader to open up interesting interdisciplinary pathways.

To further aid your reading, lists of glossary terms and people mentioned are included at the end of this book (these are indicated by an asterisk [*] throughout) – as well as a list of works cited.

Macat has worked with the University of Cambridge to identify the elements of critical thinking and understand the ways in which six different skills combine to enable effective thinking.
Three allow us to fully understand a problem; three more give us the tools to solve it. Together, these six skills make up the **PACIER** model of critical thinking. They are:

ANALYSIS – understanding how an argument is built
EVALUATION – exploring the strengths and weaknesses of an argument
INTERPRETATION – understanding issues of meaning

CREATIVE THINKING – coming up with new ideas and fresh connections
PROBLEM-SOLVING – producing strong solutions
REASONING – creating strong arguments

To find out more, visit **WWW.MACAT.COM.**

CRITICAL THINKING AND *CONFESSIONS*

Primary critical thinking skill: REASONING
Secondary critical thinking skill: CREATIVE THINKING

St. Augustine's *Confessions* is one of the most important works in the history of literature and Christian thought. Written around 397, when Augustine was the Christian bishop of Hippo (in modern-day Algeria), the *Confessions* were designed both to spiritually educate those who already shared Augustine's faith, and to convert those who did not. Augustine did this through the original maneuver of writing what is now recognized as being the first Western autobiography – letting readers share in his own experiences of youth, sin, and eventual conversion.

The *Confessions* are a perfect example of using reasoning to subtly bring readers around to a particular point of view – with Augustine inviting them to accompany him on his own spiritual journey towards God so they could make their own conversion. Carefully structured, the *Confessions* run from describing the first 43 years of Augustine's life in North Africa and Italy, to discussing the nature of memory, before moving on to analyzing the Bible itself. In order, the sections form a carefully structured argument, moving from the personal to the philosophical to the contemplative. In the hundreds of years since they were first published, they have persuaded hundreds of thousands of readers to recognize towards the same God that Augustine himself worshipped.

ABOUT THE AUTHOR OF THE ORIGINAL WORK

St. Augustine of Hippo was born in the Roman city of Thagaste, in modern-day Algeria, in 354. As a young man, he was a respected teacher of rhetoric—the art of persuasion—but he would eventually embark on an intellectual and spiritual journey that would lead him to become bishop of Hippo (today the Algerian coastal city of Annaba), as well as one of the most influential of all Catholic theologians and philosophers.

Augustine's success stemmed from his ability to combine rigorous philosophical ideas with the everyday concerns of the Church, and his writings are still relevant for many academic disciplines and Christians today. Augustine died in Hippo in 430.

ABOUT THE AUTHOR OF THE ANALYSIS

Dr Jonathan Teubner holds a PhD in intellectual history from the University of Cambridge, focusing on the reception of St Augustine. He is currently Associate Director of the Initiative on Religion, Politics and Conflict at the University of Virginia.

ABOUT MACAT

GREAT WORKS FOR CRITICAL THINKING

Macat is focused on making the ideas of the world's great thinkers accessible and comprehensible to everybody, everywhere, in ways that promote the development of enhanced critical thinking skills.

It works with leading academics from the world's top universities to produce new analyses that focus on the ideas and the impact of the most influential works ever written across a wide variety of academic disciplines. Each of the works that sit at the heart of its growing library is an enduring example of great thinking. But by setting them in context – and looking at the influences that shaped their authors, as well as the responses they provoked – Macat encourages readers to look at these classics and game-changers with fresh eyes. Readers learn to think, engage and challenge their ideas, rather than simply accepting them.

'Macat offers an amazing first-of-its-kind tool for interdisciplinary learning and research. Its focus on works that transformed their disciplines and its rigorous approach, drawing on the world's leading experts and educational institutions, opens up a world-class education to anyone.'

Andreas Schleicher
Director for Education and Skills, Organisation for Economic Co-operation and Development

'Macat is taking on some of the major challenges in university education … They have drawn together a strong team of active academics who are producing teaching materials that are novel in the breadth of their approach.'

Prof Lord Broers,
former Vice-Chancellor of the University of Cambridge

'The Macat vision is exceptionally exciting. It focuses upon new modes of learning which analyse and explain seminal texts which have profoundly influenced world thinking and so social and economic development. It promotes the kind of critical thinking which is essential for any society and economy. This is the learning of the future.'

Rt Hon Charles Clarke, former UK Secretary of State for Education

'The Macat analyses provide immediate access to the critical conversation surrounding the books that have shaped their respective discipline, which will make them an invaluable resource to all of those, students and teachers, working in the field.'

Professor William Tronzo, University of California at San Diego

WAYS IN TO THE TEXT

KEY POINTS

- Augustine of Hippo (354–430 C.E.) was a Christian bishop and theologist*—someone engaged in the systematic study of the nature of God.

- His book *Confessions* is an autobiography. It focuses on the events of Augustine's life that led to his conversion to Christianity.

- Likely one of the first autobiographies written in the West, *Confessions* is intensely personal and introspective.

Who Was Augustine?

Augustine of Hippo, author of *Confessions* (c. 397 C.E.), was born in 354 C.E. to a rising middle-class family in Thagaste, a Roman city in modern-day Algeria. Augustine was a talented student, and with the help of a wealthy local patron, he attended schools for rhetoric* (the use of persuasive language) in Carthage (a city in what is today Tunisia). After his education, he taught rhetoric, and he quickly became respected and successful. Over the course of his career, he taught in Thagaste, Carthage, Rome, and the city of Milan.

When he was young, Augustine dedicated much of his time to philosophical and religious searching. As told in *Confessions,* Augustine joined the Manichaeans,* a religious sect that subscribed to a materialist* philosophy (that is, they believed the world had been created from preexisting matter). He also became interested in Neoplatonic* philosophy, which had been developed out of the work of the Greek philosopher Plato,* arguably the most influential philosopher in Western history. Neoplatonic philosophy maintained that the soul was engaged in a mystical quest toward union with God.

Finally, in a garden in Milan, Augustine converted to Christianity and abandoned his career in rhetoric to practice asceticism* (training the body to overcome its desires so that the soul has control). He became a theologist and a church leader, and was eventually made bishop of the city of Hippo—today the Algerian coastal city of Annaba.

Augustine was the most prolific theological writer of his time, and he enjoyed widespread fame as a teacher and preacher. The first theologian to write in Latin, he is today considered among the most important thinkers in the history of Western Christianity. He died in 430 C.E. in Hippo.

What Does *Confessions* Say?

Augustine's *Confessions* tells the story of Augustine's coming of age and spiritual journey to God. To do this, the text combines episodes from Augustine's "outer life" (concerning family, career, and friendships) with episodes from his "inner life" (concerning spiritual growth and psychological change). In this way, readers should see it both as an autobiography and a spiritual memoir.

Moreover, *Confessions* is a work of theology; it includes biblical interpretation and philosophical speculation. Augustine introduces readers to his concept of divine grace, which he defined as how God acts to affect his life, continually arranging events in order to bring Augustine to Him. For example, over the course of his life, Augustine converted to the Christian Manichaean sect, to pagan philosophy (roughly, non–Christian philosophy), and finally to Catholicism* (a sect that, during this time, was defined by their belief in the Holy

Trinity—God, His son Jesus Christ,* and the Holy Spirit). Augustine believed that God had guided him toward these conversions.

For Augustine, then, salvation is neither a gift nor a revelation; instead, it is God working through human decisions and circumstances—or God's grace, as he calls it. Augustine's account shows how humans can be both free and exist in relationship to an all-powerful, all-knowing, God.

Augustine's story is full of psychological and spiritual insights. He is also remarkably attentive to feelings of guilt, shame, pride, and the desire for acceptance. Contemporary readers are often surprised that so many of Augustine's psychological experiences still ring true. Today's readers can also find meaning in the way Augustine sees God reflected in all individual experience.

Confessions shows us how to integrate religion and spirituality. It is a statement about what it means to be human, and shows that human experience does not end with the five senses.

Why Does *Confessions* Matter?

Confessions remains relevant more than 1600 years after it was written on account of its innovative combination of theology and autobiography, and for the vision of grace that it offers. The book has been translated into over 100 languages, and has influenced disciplines across the humanities and social sciences. It would be impossible to calculate how many times it has been cited, reprinted, or mentioned in print. The great German historian and theologian Adolf von Harnack* said that the language of *Confessions* has become our language, its spiritual insights have become our insights, and its problems have become our problems.[1] Indeed, *Confessions* is regarded as the definitive statement of Western Christianity outside the Bible. If today's university students read only one book from the Christian literary tradition, it is likely to be *Confessions*.

Furthermore, Augustine is considered a literary genius for his ability to express his anxieties and yearnings. Prior to the emergence in the sixteenth century of humanism*—a philosophical movement that emphasized the possibilities of human achievement and knowledge—we find few biographical accounts in Western literature that rival Augustine's candor and psychological insight; *Confessions* has remained important because it shows how people understand their own motivations and spirituality.

Some of the important thinkers and writers influenced by *Confessions* include Boethius,* a sixth-century Roman philosopher and statesman; the Florentine poet Dante Alighieri,* whose *Divine Comedy* is still among the most important works written in Italian; the English poet and author of *Canterbury Tales* Geoffrey Chaucer;* the influential French philosopher René Descartes;* the Swiss philosopher and writer Jean-Jacques Rousseau;* and the poet and playwright Johann Wolfgang von Goethe,* one of Germany's most celebrated cultural figures.

Confessions continues to be influential today. Readers can see it reflected in the work of such important figures as Joseph Ratzinger,* who served as Pope Benedict XVI from 2005 to 2013, and the former Archbishop of Canterbury Rowan Williams.*

Confessions has also long been of interest to academics. In the nineteenth and twentieth centuries, Augustine's self-reflective narrative style became significant for those studying philosophy and theology because it informed important debates about such major topics as time, narrative, and the self. Though academics very rarely write in the deeply personal and psychologically inquisitive style of *Confessions*, the book is still important because of the works it influenced, and because it offers a window into the spiritual and theological impulses of Western Christianity.

NOTES

1   Adolf von Harnack, *Augustin's Confessionen: ein Vortrag* (Giessen: Ricker'sche Buchhandlung, 1888).

SECTION 1
INFLUENCES

MODULE 1
THE AUTHOR AND THE
HISTORICAL CONTEXT

KEY POINTS

- Written in the fourth century, *Confessions* (c. 397 C.E.) is a foundational work of Western literature and theology.

- *Confessions* is a creative account of Augustine's inner life, his development from youth to middle age, and his conversion to Christianity.

- Augustine's conversion to Christianity was influenced by Platonism,* a philosophy based on the teachings of the Greek philosopher Plato* that emphasized the pursuit of wisdom. Platonism reflects the fourth-century Roman interest in knowledge and asceticism* (the practice of denying physical desires to give the mind power over the body).

Why Read This Text?

Augustine's *Confessions* (c. 397 C.E.) is one of the most influential works in Western literature. It is important historically, as it tells readers about the concerns of the fourth-century Catholic* Church (still today one of the two principal branches of the Christian faith), but it also speaks to the enduring theological and spiritual problems of human life.

The book's title has a double meaning.[1] First, it catalogues and reflects eloquently on Augustine's sins. Second, it describes how Augustine came to praise God and what that praise consists of. In this sense, *Confessions* is a thirteen-book prayer. It is known for its poetic prose and its penetrating psychological insight.

❝ I had become to myself a great puzzle. ❞

Augustine, *Confessions*

Augustine's account is an important contribution to theological and philosophical thought. The book is often considered the first autobiography,[2] and Augustine's depiction of his own inner experience went on to influence medieval theologians. Similarly, his use of the first person (writing from the perspective of "I") was taken up by René Descartes* and Jean-Jacques Rousseau,*[3] two important philosophers associated with the Enlightenment* (a major Western philosophical movement from the seventeenth to nineteenth centuries that emphasized reason, individualism, and resistance to traditional authority).

Author's Life

Augustine was born in 354 C.E. in Thagaste, a Roman city in North Africa, to a middle-class family. A wealthy local patron helped him receive a good education in Carthage's schools of rhetoric* (the use of language to persuade, inspire, and inform one's audience). He went on to teach rhetoric in North Africa in the cities of Thagaste and Carthage, and later in Rome and Milan.

Augustine gained his post in Milan because of his contacts in the Manichaeans,* a religious sect popular among young intellectuals that subscribed to a materialist* philosophy (according to which God had created the world out of preexisting matter). They viewed salvation as learning to tell "good" matter from "evil" matter (some Manichaeans, for example, believed that alcohol, as bad matter, was to be avoided).

It was here, however, that Augustine met Ambrose,* the bishop of Milan, who encouraged him to engage intellectually with the Christian Scriptures. Ambrose was also a thoroughgoing Platonist*—

that is, he subscribed to a non–materialist* philosophy, influenced by the work of the ancient Greek philosopher Plato, that valued abstraction and spirituality above physical matter. The Platonist ideas that Augustine learned through Ambrose would eventually liberate him from the materialism of the Manichaeans, which (he came to believe) could not truly lead him to God. Although Augustine would come to question some of Platonism's teachings, many of its assumptions remained important to him for the rest of his life.

One important question he sought to answer was that of authority: what sort of authority was worthwhile from a Platonic perspective?[4] The problem was that, on one hand, nothing could be accepted as authoritative simply because someone said so. But, on the other hand, Plato himself became such an authority that much of Platonist philosophy was simply a commentary on his teachings. Augustine wanted to know when it was acceptable to learn from an authority like Plato, and when one must reason on one's own. He eventually found an answer in Jesus Christ,* who as the Incarnate*—that is, God in the flesh—was both man and supreme authority. He thus converted to Catholicism,* the religion of his mother Monica.* (At that time Catholicism was a sect of Christianity defined by its belief in the Holy Trinity: God, His son Jesus Christ, and the Holy Spirit.)

Having arrived at this answer and converted, Augustine became a theologian, and eventually a bishop. It is the series of events that led to this career that *Confessions* focuses on; the book describes his philosophical, psychological, and spiritual journey to conversion.[5] In one respect, *Confessions* could be said to describe how Augustine reconciled Christianity with Platonism.

Author's Background

Augustine wrote *Confessions* while living in Hippo Regius (present-day Annaba, Algeria). While he did not have access to a major library, he was able to consult Christian and Jewish Scriptures and writers who identified with Neoplatonism* (a philosophy developed from Platonism that held that the soul was engaged in a mystical quest toward union with God). Scholars continue to debate the influences on *Confessions*, but most agree that Augustine drew from the Greek philosopher Plotinus,* founder of Neoplatonism, and Scripture (both the Old and New Testaments from the Christian Bible).

In addition to his Platonism, Augustine was a Nicene Christian:* he believed that Jesus was the divine Son of God, who, with God Himself and the Holy Spirit, made up the Trinity.[6] There is some scholarly disagreement about whether Nicene Christianity or Platonism was more important to Augustine.[7]

Confessions also stems from the cultural context in which it was written. During Augustine's time, elite members of society belonged to philosophical schools of wisdom*—schools formed during the Roman Empire to teach followers both a philosophy and a way of life. This often included a commitment to asceticism, or the practice of denying bodily urges.[8] In Augustine's case, turning to his mother's Catholicism was a commitment both to Christian ascetical life and to the authority of Christ. In *Confessions,* he comes to believe that he has been searching for Christ from the beginning.

NOTES

1   Joseph Ratzinger, "Originalität und Überlieferung in Augustins Begriff der *confessio," Revue Des Études Augustiniennes et Patristiques* 3, no. 4 (1957), 375–92.

2   Paula Fredriksen, "The *Confessions* as Autobiography," in Mark Vessey, ed. *A Companion to Augustine* (Oxford: Blackwell, 2012), 87–98.

3   James Wetzel, "Crisis Mentalities: Augustine after Descartes," in *Parting Knowledge: Essays after Augustine* (Eugene, OR: Cascade Books, 2013), 28–44; Ann Hartle, *The Modern Self in Rousseau's Confessions: A Reply to St. Augustine* (Notre Dame: University of Notre Dame Press, 1983).

4   Saint Augustine, *Confessions*, trans. Henry Chadwick (Oxford: Oxford University Press, 1991), 7.7.11.

5   Possidius, "The Life of St. Augustine," in *Early Christian Biographies*, ed. Roy J. Deferrari (Washington, DC: Catholic University of America Press, 1952).

6   Lewis Ayres, *Nicaea and its Legacy* (Oxford: Oxford University Press, 2004), 366.

7   Pierre Courcelle, *Recherches sur les Confessions de Saint Augustin: Nouvelle édition augmentée et illustrée* (Paris: Éditions E. de Boccard, 1968); Robert J. O'Connell, *St. Augustine's Confessions: The Odyssey of Soul* (Cambridge, MA: Belknap Harvard University Press, 1969); James J. O'Donnell, *Augustine Confessions*, vol. 1, *Introduction and Text* (Oxford: Oxford University Press, 1992).

8   Pierre Hadot, *Philosophy as a Way of Life* (Oxford: Blackwell Publishing, 1995), 126.

MODULE 2
ACADEMIC CONTEXT

KEY POINTS

- In Augustine's context—the Roman Empire in the fourth century—religious life was inseparable from philosophical thought.

- When people joined schools of wisdom* at that time, they submitted to teaching authority and to asceticism* (the practice of training to give the soul control over the body and its desires).

- *Confessions* tells the story of Augustine's pursuit of wisdom as informed by early Christian beliefs and Neoplatonism* (a philosophy founded on the belief that the soul was engaged in a quest toward union with God).

The Work in its Context

In the world of Augustine, the author of *Confessions*, religion was a vital part of everyday existence and philosophical thought. The pursuit of wisdom consisted of both rationalization (the pursuit of truth) and purification (the pursuit of a pure life). In the late fourth century, many philosophers believed that in order to pursue truth, one first learned to live purely. This is the challenge that Augustine's *Confessions* takes up: it describes one man's search, informed by ancient philosophical traditions, for wisdom.[1]

A variety of forms of Christianity existed in the Roman Empire in the fourth century, including those followed by both Manichaeans* (a sect that thrived between the third and seventh centuries) and Catholics.* Augustine, who had been baptized as an infant, belonged to both these at different times. Christianity was therefore an

> ❝ In the ordinary course of study, I lighted upon a certain book of Cicero, whose language, though not his heart, almost all admire. This book of his contains an exhortation to philosophy, and is called *Hortensius*. This book, in truth, changed my affections, and turned my prayers to Yourself, O Lord, and made me have other hopes and desires. ❞
>
> Augustine, *Confessions*

importance influence throughout his life.

At the same time, Platonic* philosophy, which emphasized the abstract over the material, was being further developed by Neoplatonic thinkers; Augustine himself was significantly influenced by the writings of Plotinus,* the Greek philosopher who founded Neoplatonism.[2]

Overview of the Field

Two issues were particularly important to philosophers in the Roman Empire in the fourth century: authority and asceticism.[3] Augustine's search for wisdom was essentially a search for authority. This did not mean that Augustine submitted to authority uncritically; rather, he committed to thinking inside the tenets of a tradition. He found this tradition after meeting Ambrose,* the bishop of Milan, who introduced Augustine to Christianity as the one "true philosophy."

Augustine's commitment also involved adopting certain ascetic practices, such as sexual denial, communal living, and educating the community's members. This was not unusual for his time; various philosophical traditions offered adherents strategies for controlling their physical urges—that is, strategies for purification. For example, Porphyry,* an anti-Christian Platonist writer, also renounced sex and adopted a specific diet. In this way, Augustine shares a similar background with many other intellectuals across the Roman Empire; this is reflected in his *Confessions.*

Academic Influences

As he relates in the work, at the age of 16 Augustine read *Hortentius* (*On Philosophy,* 45 B.C.E.) by the famous Roman orator and politician Cicero.* Though *Hortentius* is now unfortunately lost, Augustine credits it with inspiring the pursuit of wisdom that he maintained through his experiences with various philosophical and religious sects, and, in part, for motivating his conversion to Catholicism.[4]

One experience that informed Augustine's thinking was his time as a "hearer" in the Manichaean sect. During those 10 years, Augustine became increasingly dissatisfied with how the Manichaeans answered the problem of evil,* or the question of why evil is permitted by a supreme being or God.

In *Confessions,* Augustine writes that he was liberated from Manichaeism by reading Platonist books, as well as through the ideas of Academicians* (a school of philosophy marked by its skepticism about whether anything could be considered undoubtedly true).[5] Augustine was also guided by Ambrose, the bishop of Milan, who was a deeply Platonist Christian who modeled how one might intellectually engage with the Christian Scriptures.

Although Augustine eventually came to question certain Platonist teachings, his Christian thought was powerfully shaped by Platonist philosophy. It is worth noting that in the fourth century, Platonist thought underpinned much of daily life in the Roman Empire, and informed many schools of philosophy.

Eventually, Augustine returned to the Catholic Church and was ultimately consecrated as a bishop. This return is the central narrative of *Confessions.*

NOTES

1 Pierre Hadot, *Philosophy as a Way of Life* (Oxford: Blackwell Publishing, 1995), 126.

2 John Peter Kenney, *Mystical Monotheism: A Study in Ancient Platonic Theology* (Eugene, OR: Wipf and Stock, 1991), 150.

3 Conrad Leyser, *Authority and Asceticism from Augustine to Gregory the Great* (Oxford: Oxford University Press, 2000).

4 Saint Augustine, *Confessions*, trans. Henry Chadwick (Oxford: Oxford University Press, 1991), 3.4.7.

5 Augustine, *Confessions*, 6.9.18.

MODULE 3
THE PROBLEM

KEY POINTS

- One important issue of fourth-century Roman culture was how people attained wisdom. Augustine believed this question should take the form: "How can I come to know God?"

- Augustine answered this question by drawing on the Platonic* idea that evil was not material, but spiritual. He concluded that ultimately, people needed to look inward to recognize their own sins.

- Augustine encountered Platonic Christianity through Ambrose,* Bishop of Milan; he was, however, more critical of Platonic thought than Ambrose.

Core Question

Augustine's *Confessions* begins with a question: if we call on God before we come to know God, how can we be sure that we are truly calling on God and not something that only seems like Him?

To answer this question, Augustine drew on Platonist philosophy, which equated finding wisdom with finding happiness. Christians influenced by Platonism* were able to adapt this understanding of wisdom to their own spiritual purpose—namely, the pressing question of *how* one comes to call on and know God.

Today, this seems like an epistemological* question—a question concerning the nature of knowledge. Comparatively, to Augustine and his fourth-century readers, it was much more than an intellectual inquiry. It involved the senses and emotions, too. The question of whether or not one must know God to call on Him, then, takes Augustine on a journey that is intellectual, emotional, moral, and

Macat Analysis of Augustine's *Confessions*

> ❝ You stir man to take pleasure in praising you, because you have made us for yourself, and our heart is restless until it rests in you. Grant me Lord to know and understand which comes first—to call upon you or to praise you, and whether knowing you precedes calling upon you. But who calls upon you when he does not know you? ❞
>
> Augustine, *Confessions*

spiritual.

Augustine writes about this in a way that was innovative—through describing his personal experience. That said, the journey itself was not new. This question was supremely important to fourth-century Christians, especially because Roman culture offered so many different strategies for finding wisdom or "happiness."[1] We can more fully understand this by considering the ancient philosophical language used in this discussion.

The English word "happiness" does not have quite the same meaning as its Roman equivalent: *eudaemonia,** which describes how much a person has employed his or her talents and enjoyed life's gifts. So, while "happiness" might describe an immediate emotional state, *eudaemonia* refers to how a person has lived his or her life.

The Participants

Augustine's main concern in *Confessions* is to tell the reader how he came to know God. He does this through writing about conversion, ascent* (the soul's journey to God), Christ's work, and pilgrimage. These ideas were supported by his concepts of humility and grace, and to a less obvious extent, by love and God's warnings to people concerning their desires.

One other important idea is the problem of evil:* how can evil exist in a world created by an all-powerful God? Augustine and his contemporaries understood this question as concerning the soul. Augustine believed that the soul was a kind of microcosm—a model in miniature—of the universe. Therefore, while his personal evil was only a speck in the greater problem of evil, examining his own morality could tell him something about morality in general.[2]

This is the problem to which most of Augustine's early work criticizing the Manichaean* religion was dedicated. Augustine believed that the Manichaeans' materialism,* which held that the world had been wholly created from preexisting matter, did not fully explain what "evil" was. This is why he turned to Platonism,* which taught that evil was immaterial*—that is, roughly, spiritual.

In turn, this led him to reflect on the soul's journey toward God, a process he labeled "ascent." While these exercises helped Augustine understand evil, he did not think they showed him how to purify himself:

"It is one thing from a wooded summit to catch a glimpse of the homeland of peace and not to find a way to it … It is another thing to hold on to the way that leads there, defended by the protection of the heavenly emperor."[3]

Augustine, then, examined the evil that was hidden in his moral choices. This was an important exercise in humility, and it helped him recognize the grace required for redemption; grace, according to Augustine, is God's presence in everyday human actions. Writing and publishing *Confessions,* an account of his sins, is an act of humility. Readers can see the text as a dialogue between the soul and God about good and evil.

The Contemporary Debate

While Augustine is widely known as a Platonist Christian, it is important to recognize that he was also critical of some Platonist assumptions. Certainly he was less committed to Platonism than was, for example, Ambrose, the bishop of Milan. Ambrose tried to incorporate into Christian thought many ideas that he saw as truthful from the pagan (non-Christian) philosophy.

Augustine was more inquisitive: entire paragraphs of *Confessions* are made up of questions. These often lead to unexpected places. One example of this occurs in Book 10, in which Augustine reflects on his conversion, and a series of questions leads him "to the fields and vast palaces of memory."[4]

But the questions all eventually lead back to one particular line of inquiry: where did Augustine's knowledge of God come from? Was it always there? And if it had always been there, how had he not known it?

Augustine did not agree with the Platonic idea that people could attain purification, or knowledge of God, on their own. For Augustine, people needed divine assistance—"grace"—to truly know Him.

NOTES

1   Jean-Marie Salamito, *Les virtuoses et la Multitude: Aspects sociaux de la controverse entre Augustin et les pélagiens* (Grenoble: Éditions Jérôme Millon, 2005), 29ff.

2   John M. Rist, *Augustine: Ancient Thought Baptized* (Cambridge: Cambridge University Press, 1994), 92–5.

3   Saint Augustine, *Confessions*, trans. Henry Chadwick (Oxford: Oxford University Press, 1991), 7.21.27.

4   Augustine, *Confessions*, 10.8.12.

MODULE 4
THE AUTHOR'S CONTRIBUTION

KEY POINTS

* The form of Augustine's *Confessions* was original in that it was a combination of autobiography and theology. It also offered new theological* ideas.

* Augustine's account of how the soul knew God came from Neoplatonism* and from his reading of the part of the New Testament known as the Epistles (Letters) of Paul*— especially Paul's Epistle to the Romans.

* Augustine's understanding of divine grace emphasizes that God affects the events of people's lives.

Author's Aims

In *Confessions,* Augustine has two main aims. First, he wanted to establish his authority as the new bishop of Hippo. It was well known that Augustine converted from the religion of Manichaeism* to the Catholic* sect of Christianity during his time in Italy. While this won him support from Catholic bishops, most Christians living in North Africa in 397 were Donatists*—a sect that believed their version of Christianity was the only valid version. *Confessions* was therefore a preemptive defense against those, like the Donatists, who doubted his authority in his new position.

Second, in addition to proving his authority, *Confessions* is a creative, theological work in which Augustine confesses his sins and praises God.

Confessions is therefore both argumentative, in that it defends the writer's reputation, and spiritual, in its explanation of theological ideas through the lens of Augustine's journey toward understanding.

> ❝ Late have I loved you, beauty so ancient and so new: late have I loved you. And see, you were within and I was in the external world and sought you there, and in my unlovely state I plunged into those lovely created things which you made. You were with me, and I was not with you. ❞
>
> Augustine, *Confessions*

These two aims are reflected in the structure of *Confessions*. The work is divided into a narrative portion (Books 1–9), in which Augustine recounts the events of his life that led to conversion, and a speculative portion (Books 10–13), in which he praises God.

Though there is a great deal of scholarly debate about *Confessions,* most agree these two parts cohere around the idea of the soul's ascension toward God, a concept that Augustine probably first encountered through his reading of Neoplatonic texts.[1] Scholars also agree that these two accounts, biographical and scriptural, were structured according to understanding of education in fourth-century philosophy.[2] One point on which scholars do not agree, however, is whether Augustine was influenced more by the intellectual rigor of the Greek philosopher Plotinus,* or the ascetic* practices of Plotinus's student Porphyry,* a philosopher and critic of Christianity.

Approach

Augustine's account of the soul's ascent* to God in *Confessions* was a response to his Neoplatonic reading and to Scripture. He had begun to explore this subject in earlier work, gradually integrating these two influences.

Augustine wrote his *Soliloquia* ("Soliloquies," c. 380), for example, in the form of an internal dialogue. In it, he poses questions and answers that lead toward knowledge of God and the soul. He also draws on the book of the Bible known as Psalms.

In *De Vera Religione* ("On True Religion," c. 390), Augustine begins to use the language of Christian Scripture in his description of the soul. He also explores the nature of Scripture itself. This approach was more fully articulated in *Ad Simplicianum* ("On Simplician," 396), when Augustine was beginning to think seriously about the Biblical letters of Paul. Here, he was able to describe grace as always having been at work in him, and therefore necessary for knowing God.[3]

In these three texts, then, readers can see the origin of the core issue of *Confessions*. In *Soliloquia*, Augustine discovers that people come to know God through their souls; in *De Vera Religione*, he uses Scripture to help him articulate the mysterious movements of the soul; and in *Ad Simplicianum*, he becomes aware that God has always been at work in his life, arranging events so as to lead Augustine's soul to God.

Contribution in Context

Augustine's use of Scripture, his description of the soul's knowledge of God, and his concept of grace represent a shift away from the Christian Platonism* of Ambrose,* Bishop of Milan, who greatly influenced Augustine. One major difference between the two was that Augustine believed that God's grace affected all aspects of human life.

Because he emphasized God's action, Augustine's account may appear to marginalize the importance of human will. Augustine's intention, however, was not to diminish the role of personal choice, but to show that God cooperated with human action.[4] More specifically, Augustine believed that God's grace affected the events of his life in order to lead his soul to God. This understanding of God as cooperative would eventually make Augustine a major figure of Latin Christian theology. In this way, *Confessions* anticipates later developments both in Augustine's work and in Latin theology.

Augustine's *Confessions* is also innovative because of its unusual literary form. The book is generally regarded as the first autobiography, and it also creatively drew on scriptural, polemical (strongly-stated argument), and theological writing styles.[5] One achievement of *Confessions* is that, in bringing together so many different strands of Augustine's own life, it illustrates many of the tensions of late fourth-century Latin theology.

NOTES

1   Saint Augustine, *Confessions*, trans. Henry Chadwick (Oxford: Oxford University Press, 1991), 7.10.16; see also Peter King, "Augustine's Anti-Platonist Ascents," in William E. Mann, ed. *Augustine's* Confessions: *Philosophy in Autobiography* (Oxford: Oxford University Press, 2014), 6–27.

2   Robert O'Connell, *St. Augustine's Confessions: The Odyssey of Soul* (New York: Fordham University Press, 1989); Frederick Van Fleteren, "Augustine's Ascent of the Soul in Book VII of the Confessions: A Reconsideration," *Augustinian Studies* 5 (1974): 29–72.

3   Augustine, *Ad simplicianum* 1.2.21, in *Augustine: Earlier Writings*, ed. J. H. S. Burleigh (Philadelphia: The Westminster Press, 1953).

4   James Wetzel, "The Alleged Importance of Free Choice: Augustine on *Liberum Arbitrium*," in *Parting Knowledge: Essays after Augustine* (Eugene, OR: Cascade Books, 2013), 45–57.

5   Erich Auerbach, *Literary Language and its Public in Late Latin Antiquity and in the Middle Ages*, trans. Ralph Manheim (Princeton, NJ: Princeton University Press, 1965), 25.

SECTION 2
IDEAS

MODULE 5
MAIN IDEAS

KEY POINTS

- Augustine's key themes are conversion, ascent* (the soul's journey to God), Jesus Christ,* and pilgrimage.
- These help illustrate his primary ideas about humility and grace.
- Augustine presents his conversion to Christianity as a personal narrative.

Key Themes

Augustine's *Confessions* describes how he comes to know God. There are four recurring themes that support his account: conversion, ascent, Christ, and pilgrimage.

Augustine comes to see his *conversions*—from one philosophical school to another, from the Manichaean* sect, and eventually to Catholic Christianity—as ordered by God. The theme of *ascent* concerns the soul's journey to know God. Augustine eventually arrives at the belief that knowledge of God must occur between God and the soul. When Augustine recognizes God in *Christ*—understood as God-become-human—he begins to understand that one must first humbly descend (as Christ did, in becoming human) in order to ascend to God. *Pilgrimage* is the journey to God that Augustine narrates, and which the reader is invited to join.

Two concepts central to the text are humility and grace. Humility is demonstrated in Christ's taking human form (the Incarnation)* and it is also required for Augustine to confess his sins so that his soul may seek God. Seeking, however, is only possible because of God's grace—

> **66** I heard a voice from a nearby house chanting as if it might be a boy or a girl (I do not know which), saying and repeating over and over again 'Pick up and read, pick up and read.' ... I hurried back to the place Alypius was sitting. There I had put down the book of the apostle [Paul] when I got up. I seized it, opened it and in silence read the first passage my eyes lit: 'Not in riots and drunken parties, not in eroticism and indecencies, not in strife and rivalry, but put on the Lord Jesus Christ and make no provision for the flesh in its lusts. **99**
>
> Augustine, *Confessions*

that is, God's role in ordering the events of Augustine's life.

Exploring the Ideas

The first six books of *Confessions* are an account of the conversions that were most formative for Augustine: to philosophy, to Manichaeism, and to Platonism.* In Book 7, when he recounts his conversion from Manichaeism to Platonism, Augustine describes three attempted ascents. Though the first two fail, the third seems at first to succeed:

"And so step by step I ascended from bodies to the soul which perceives through the body, and from there to its inward force ... from there again I ascended to the power of reasoning ... this power, which in myself I found to be mutable, raised itself to the level of its own intelligence, and led my thinking out of the ruts of habit." [1]

Something still seems lacking for Augustine, however, as he reflects: "But I did not possess the strength to keep my vision fixed." [2]

In Books 7 and 8, Augustine reasons that what is lacking—why he cannot sustain his vision—is Christ. Platonism only allows him to glimpse the truth, whereas a Christ-centered devotion permits him to fully see Truth.

Augustine's depiction of this final conversion in Book 9 is famous. It occurs in a garden in Milan while he reflects on Scripture with his mother. Here, ascent is described as a kind "searching together in the presence of truth which is you yourself."[3] This conversion is where Augustine first experiences beatitude,* an immediate knowledge of God: "And while we talked and panted after it, we touched it in some small degree by a moment of total concentration of the heart. And we sighed and left behind us 'the first fruits of the Spirit' bound to that higher world, as we returned to the noise of our human speech."[4]

Augustine realizes that he must take on the humility that Christ demonstrated in the Incarnation (literally, "becoming flesh").[5] The pilgrimage, therefore, is the process of becoming Christlike—a process that will not be complete until the afterlife, when (according to Augustine) Christians will be made perfect. As Augustine puts it: "If only it could last, and other visions of a vastly inferior kind could be withdrawn!"[6] The final Books (10–13), especially Book 13, are an account of how this pilgrimage structures Christian life.

Language and Expression

Confessions might be confusing for those not used to reading theological literature. It is worth keeping in mind that it is not just a summary of Augustine's philosophical positions. It is also personal: Augustine's narrative is an expression of his soul's relationship with God, and he invites readers to accompany him and feel the effects of his confession. Augustine's training in rhetoric*—the use of language to convince or provoke to action—would have given him many techniques for doing this in ways that would delight, persuade, and move readers.

We should not, then, see *Confessions* as strictly academic. One of Augustine's goals is to dramatize his central ideas (that is, his understanding of conversion, ascent, Christ, pilgrimage, humility, and grace), so that these ideas appear to emerge naturally from his life's story—and be relevant to his readers' lives, too. People have long enjoyed reading *Confessions*, and this means that Augustine has had the opportunity to teach readers through the ages.

NOTES

1 Saint Augustine, *Confessions*, trans. Henry Chadwick (Oxford: Oxford University Press, 1991), 7.17.23.

2 Saint Augustine, *Confessions*, 7.17.23.

3 Augustine, *Confessions,* 9.10.23.

4 Augustine, *Confessions,* 9.10.24.

5 Augustine, *Confessions*, 7.18.24.

6 Augustine, *Confessions*, 9.10.25.

MODULE 6
SECONDARY IDEAS

KEY POINTS

- The concept of God's love for humanity is one of the text's most important secondary ideas.

- Another is that God intervenes in people's lives by warning them about their desires.

- Augustine's emphasis that Christ healed the relationship between God and the human soul—or Christology,* as he called it—has sometimes been overlooked.

Other Ideas

As we have seen, in *Confessions* Augustine demonstrates how he comes to know God. His book is a narrative that relies on the concepts of conversion, ascent,* Jesus Christ's* work, and pilgrimage; the movement from sin to righteousness, sickness to health, and ignorance to knowledge, requires humility and grace, both of which should be understood as divine interventions into human life. But the journey is not just about the work God does; human action is important, too.

Two ideas about human action, love and admonition, were particularly important to Augustine.

Augustine takes the Incarnation,* the Christian doctrine that the son of God took human form, as a prime demonstration of God's love. He believes that as a result, all humans are required to love God in return.

Admonitions—or warnings—play a special role in *Confessions,* since they direct Augustine's actions at critical moments. Some of these admonitions are internal, such as when Augustine seems to hear

> ❝ The thirteen books of my *Confessions* refer to my evil
> or good, praise the just and good God, and stimulate the
> heart and mind of man to approach unto Him. And, as far
> as I am concerned, they wrought this in me when they
> were written, and this they still do when they are read. ❞
>
> Augustine, *Retractions*

a voice; others are external, such as when he bases a choice on something somebody else says. Augustine comes to recognize these admonitions as God's grace directing him.

Exploring the Ideas

In his youth, Augustine follows every fancy he has. These desires, he believes initially, are his biggest problem. But in *Confessions*, he comes to see the importance of desire. Desire should not be dismissed but directed properly—toward God: "For this city your pilgrim people yearn, from their leaving it to their return."[1] Augustine begins to understand love theologically when he realizes that the Incarnation is itself God's love for him.

Like humility, love both explains God's descent and is something Augustine must learn to redirect. In other words, Augustine must understand love intellectually, and as a transformative force in his life. It is critical—not only to *Confessions* but also to Augustine's work as a whole—for readers to recognize that he does not deny human desire, but instead asserts that it should be to directed to God.

Another important aspect of *Confessions* are the admonitions that Augustine experiences. For example, he experiences an admonition while reading Platonist* books: "By the Platonic books I was admonished to return into myself."[2] Augustine believes that this admonition comes neither from what the books say nor his inner desire, but from God.

Similarly, in Book 8, Augustine hears another admonition while in the garden: "pick up and read, pick up and read."[3] He sees this as an example of God affecting the material conditions of his life.

In this way, he notes that God's grace works both externally and internally by directing voices toward him (for example, from Platonist books) and in the form of his own inner voice. Augustine believes that God has been admonishing, and so directing, him all along.

Overlooked

Augustine's understanding of Christ, or Christology, has often been overlooked in studies of *Confessions.* The person of Christ plays a crucial role in Augustine's account of the relationship between God and humanity. Augustine believed, as many Christians have and still do, that Christ is God, and that Christ came down to earth as a great act of divine condescension, as if a king had decided to live with peasants. The event of the Incarnation—of God becoming human—defines love for Augustine.

This creates a difficulty in understanding Augustine's view of Christ. On the one hand, Augustine believed that belief in the Incarnation was a necessary part of Christian faith. On the other hand, however, Augustine writes in Book 7 that Platonist philosophers did not buy the idea of God becoming human,[4] and he concedes that Incarnation is impossible because of the vast metaphysical* differences—those differences going beyond the laws of nature, or physical matter itself—between God and humans.[5]

This apparent contradiction has been the subject of significant scholarly attention. Few scholars have considered that Augustine views the Incarnation as an act of healing the relationship between God and humanity.

Scholarship over Augustine's Christology has been heavily influenced by the leading German philosopher Martin Heidegger* and in particular his 1921 lectures on *Confessions*. At it happens, Heidegger does not concern himself with some of the most interesting passages on Christology of book 10, regarding them as merely decorative.[6] Heidegger's judgment has caused scholars to ignore these passages.

NOTES

1   Saint Augustine, *Confessions*, trans. Henry Chadwick (Oxford: Oxford University Press, 1991), 9.8.37.

2   Augustine, Confessions, 7.10.16.

3   Augustine, *Confessions*, 8.12.29.

4   Augustine, *Confessions*, 7.20.26.

5   John Peter Kenney, *Contemplation and Classical Christianity: A Study in Augustine* (Oxford: Oxford University Press, 2013), 68.

6   Martin Heidegger, *The Phenomenology of Religious Life*, trans. Matthias Fritsch and Jennifer Anna Gosetti-Ferencei (Bloomington, IN: Indiana University Press, 2010), 182ff.

MODULE 7
ACHIEVEMENT

KEY POINTS

- Augustine's memoir both secured his authority as a bishop and developed a Christian account of the soul's ascent* to God.

- Although *Confessions* was not immediately popular, over time it has become Augustine's best-known work.

- Modern readers may find parts of *Confessions* problematic—the way it portrays women, for example.

Assessing the Argument

There is no doubt that *Confessions* helped Augustine defend his authority as a Christian teacher. But there are many other reasons the book became—and still is—important throughout the Western world.

Augustine writes the story of his life in order to accomplish his larger theological goals. Using a narrative to confess his sins and praise God helps present Augustine as a genuine Christian, but it also provides evidence for how the soul ascends to God. That is, Augustine's own life becomes evidence for his theological argument.

While Augustine draws on Platonic* ideas, his account of ascent is fully Christian. One difference is that, unlike Platonic ascent, Christian ascent first requires a humble descent, as modeled by the Incarnation* of God in the human form of Jesus Christ.* The ascents that Augustine reports throughout *Confessions* are only tastes of the ultimate beatific* vision (that is, the immediate knowledge) of God.

While this beatific vision is the aim of *Confessions*, it is important to note that it is achieved not in this life, but in the next—after death. So, although Augustine establishes his authority as a Christian teacher and

> 66 When I first came to know you, you raised me up to make me see that what I saw is Being, and that I who saw am not yet Being. And you gave a shock to the weakness of my sight by the strong radiance of your rays, and I trembled with love and awe. And I found myself far from you in the region of dissimilarity. 99

Augustine, *Confessions*

bishop, he does so only in the course of achieving his greater goal: understanding the soul's ascent to God. Importantly, he reinvents Platonic ideas to inform this understanding.

Achievement in Context

In his own lifetime, *Confessions* was not Augustine's most popular work. He was known mostly as an intelligent defender of Catholicism,* and as a critic of smaller sects and the philosophical paganism (roughly, models of pre-Christian philosophy and religion) whose influence was beginning to dwindle.

Augustine's letters were much more widely read than his longer works. One reason for this is that educated people in the fourth century were letter-writers. Another is more practical: paper was expensive. To get a copy of Augustine's *Confessions* would have been costly. Only very wealthy people and members of powerful institutions (such as cathedral scribes) would have been able to afford *Confessions*. In addition to his letters, his contemporaries read his transcribed speeches, sermons, and polemical addresses on the hot topics of the day.[1]

Today, however, *Confessions* has become Augustine's most famous work and a classic of Western literature that influences many academic disciplines. Many fields claim it as their own (as is true of many texts written before the modern division of the disciplines). Among these are theology, philosophy, history, and classics—the study of ancient Greek and Latin literature.

To a lesser extent, fields such as literature, psychology, sociology, and political science have also demonstrated enduring interest in *Confessions*. In the social sciences, this interest comes from the historical influence that *Confessions* has had. Today's readers should note that Augustine's insights would widely be considered naïve compared with current theoretical and experimental approaches.

Limitations

While *Confessions* is extraordinarily important to theology, religious philosophy, and other disciplines, it is also subject to charges of naïvety, bigotry, and repression, especially from a psychological or sociological perspective. Augustine often bears the weight of criticisms that might be generally applied to Western Christianity.[2]

The most obviously problematic aspect of Augustine's text is the way he portrays women. While his mother, Monica,* plays an exalted role, she is mostly important because of her lack of education. Another example is Augustine's concubine, or mistress, of 13 years. After obtaining his post as a teacher of rhetoric* in Milan, she becomes a social liability, and he sends her away.[3]

It was not uncommon for men of Augustine's time to take concubines before settling on marriage, and this practice was allowed by the Catholic Church.[4] Still, readers today are likely to be troubled by Augustine's treatment and dismissal of women.

Confessions is also the subject of other scholarly discussion. For example, since the arrival of deconstructionism,* a type of critical analysis that questions whether it can ever be possible to read and understand a written text objectively, it is not clear how accurately autobiographical narratives represent the self's experience. Another issue is how one writes theology when Western readership is paradoxically uninterested in "religion" yet fascinated by "spirituality."

NOTES

1   Karla Pollmann, et al., introduction to *The Oxford Guide to the Historical Reception of Augustine* (Oxford: Oxford University Press, 2013).

2   James J. O'Donnell, "Augustine: Christianity and Society," Georgetown University, accessed August 24, 2015, http://faculty.georgetown.edu/jod/twayne/aug3.html.

3   Saint Augustine, *Confessions*, trans. Henry Chadwick (Oxford: Oxford University Press, 1991), 6.15.25.

4   Kyle Harper, *From Shame to Sin: The Christian Transformation of Sexual Morality in Late Antiquity* (Cambridge, MA: Harvard University Press, 2013).

MODULE 8
PLACE IN THE AUTHOR'S WORK

KEY POINTS

- *Confessions* represents the middle of Augustine's career: it draws on his earlier, more speculative work, and anticipates his later focus on theological controversies.

- Augustine had always been interested in how one could know God. By the time he wrote *Confessions*, his ideas had matured thanks to his reflections on the letters of the Apostle Paul* and his new understandings of sin and grace.

- *Confessions*, Augustine's best-known work, has powerfully influenced Christian theology and Western literature.

Positioning

Most scholars today agree that *Confessions* was written around 397 C.E., and that it combines Augustine's early philosophical concerns with his emerging interest in Scriptural interpretation and Church life. His philosophical interests, such as reason, memory, and metaphysics* (the branch of philosophy that deals with the nature of being itself), dominate major sections of the text (particularly Books 7 and 10). And his emphasis on Scripture and on forming a community of Christians (such as in Books 8 and 9) indicates the formation of a deepening involvement in the life of the Church.

Some aspects of *Confessions* are still up for debate, however. For example: does the book represent a turning point in Augustine's life? After all, it does seem to both reflect earlier work and anticipate his later writing. Some scholars have read *Confessions* as evidence that after becoming bishop of Hippo, Augustine's outlook fundamentally changed to that of a Church leader.[1]

> ❝ No one knows what he himself is made of, except his own spirit within him, yet there is still some part of him which remains hidden even from his own spirit; but you, Lord, know everything about a human being because you have made him ... Let me, then, confess what I know about myself, and confess too what I do not know, because what I know of myself I know only because you shed light on me, and what I do not know I shall remain ignorant about until my darkness becomes like bright noon before your face. ❞
>
> Augustine, *Confessions*

This thesis has, however, come under significant scrutiny. Most scholars today suggest that Augustine never stopped developing as a thinker: *Confessions* corrects and modifies earlier work.[2] Since *Confessions* is an account of Augustine's conversion as well as a dramatization of the intellectual and spiritual revelations that led to conversion, the question of where in his development it falls is important for understanding the work itself.

Integration

Augustine's early work is often associated with the locations in which he wrote. His earliest surviving work dates from 386, when he was on retreat at Cassiciacum, in what is today northern Italy. During this time—which was before his conversion—he wrote several philosophical dialogues that explored the nature of the good life, the problem of evil,* skepticism, and reason.

After his baptism into Catholicism* in Milan (387), Augustine returned with his friends, his son Adeodatus,* and his mother Monica* to North Africa. En route to Thagaste, they stayed in Rome, where Augustine came into contact with some ascetic* communities and learned about their practices of controlling the body's urges through self-denial, commonly of luxuries or society, so that the soul could have more control. After this point he began to write short treatises on free will, the Catholic and Manichaean* ways of life, and the soul.

When Augustine and his entourage reached Thagaste, they started a community based on the principles by which monks lived. It was during this time that Augustine's work turned toward Scripture: Augustine wrote his first of five commentaries on Genesis (the first book of the Old Testament) and continued to write on philosophical themes such as the nature of language and teaching.

Shortly after the death of his son in 390 or thereabouts, Augustine was called to be ordained as bishop of Hippo.[3] Sometime between his ordination and the writing of *Confessions*, some important changes seemed to have occurred in his theological thinking. While he was already acquainted with Scripture, he began to reflect more seriously on the writings of the Apostle Paul, author of several New Testament epistles (letters).

There is much debate over whether or not studying Paul's writing provoked a kind of "revolution" in Augustine's thought. Most scholars at least agree that there was a pronounced change in what he focused on.[4] In particular, Augustine began to think about the nature of grace and the sinful state of humanity. If most of Augustine's early work attempted to understand God and how people come to know God, then *Confessions* is a major breakthrough: Augustine announces that God's grace is the answer to these problems, as only through God's grace can the soul come to know God.

Significance

Confessions is generally credited with being the first autobiography. It also creatively incorporated genres in which Augustine had previously written, integrating scriptural, polemical (argumentative), and theological language. But perhaps its greatest achievement is that, in bringing together so many strands of Augustine's life, it explores a number of important tensions in late fourth-century Latin theology.

While more famous in his day as a Church leader and letter-writer than as the author of *Confessions*, it is now his best-known work. It is also a key text for any who wish to understand major issues in Christian thinking. In addition to its influence on Western literature, *Confessions* anticipates Augustine's later work in scriptural commentary, polemical tracts, and speculative doctrine.

Finally, Augustine's account of grace—that is, of the gift of knowing God—is especially significant because in his story, it occurs in the context of friendships, labor, and community. The idea of grace is, then, inseparable from the events and the people that populate human life.

NOTES

1   James J. O'Donnell, *Augustine, Sinner and Saint: A New Biography* (London: Profile Books Ltd, 2005).

2   Rudolf Lorenz, "Augustin," in *Religion in Geschichte Und Gegenwart* (Tübingen: Mohr Siebeck, 1957); G. S. Madec, *Saint Augustin et la Philosophie* (Paris: Études Augustiniennes, 1996); Gaetano Lettieri, *L'altro Agostino. Ermeneutica e Retorica Della Grazia Dalla Crisi Alla Metamorfosi Del De Doctrina Christiana* (Brescia: Morcelliana, 2002).

3   Saint Augustine, *Confessions,* trans. Henry Chadwick (Oxford: Oxford University Press, 1991), 9.6.14.

4   James Wetzel, *Augustine and the Limits of Virtue* (Cambridge: Cambridge University Press, 1992); Lettieri, *L'altro Agostino.*

SECTION 3
IMPACT

MODULE 9
THE FIRST RESPONSES

KEY POINTS

- While we know very little about early responses to *Confessions*, it appears that it was well received.

- Among his first readers, Augustine seems to have been widely regarded as a respected Christian teacher and saint.

- Augustine's popularity and authority was probably due to, among other things, his unusual combination of philosophical skill and his engagement with the concerns of everyday Church life.

Criticism

It is not clear what kinds of responses Augustine received after publishing *Confessions* in about 397 C.E. We can imagine that he was critiqued by his intended audiences—the Donatist* church in Hippo (an early Christian sect associated with North Africa), the Manichaeans* living in Carthage (followers of a religion that incorporated certain elements of Christian doctrine), various disciples of pagan Platonism,* and Catholics* who practiced a Christianity that was less academically rigorous, typical of North Africa at the time. But this would be speculative. No recorded critiques of *Confessions* from the period following its publication have been discovered, nor do we have any record of Augustine responding directly to a critic.

Later, in *Retractiones* ("Retractions," c. 426), in which he revisited his older works, Augustine suggests that people did receive *Confessions* well: "What others may think about them is up to them, but I know that they have pleased and do please many of the brothers a great deal."[1] Also, during an exchange of letters, Augustine sent the eminent

> ❝ In my *Confessions*, contemplate me so that you do not praise me beyond what I am; in them, believe not others about me but me myself. In them pay attention to me and see through me what I was in myself. And, if anything in me pleases you, praise there, along with me, not me but him whom I have wanted to be praised because of me. ❞
>
> Augustine, *Letter 231 to* Count Darius

Count Darius a copy, which suggests that he had not experienced any serious challenges to *Confessions*.[2] Though Augustine frequently reconsidered and revised claims he made in other earlier texts, he seems to have had nothing to retract from *Confessions*.

Responses

As Augustine's fame grew throughout the Roman Empire, his works were increasingly read and discussed among learned Christians. Augustine was well aware of this and often tried to quiet such discussions. In a sermon late in his life, he even argued against such devoted readings: "So if anybody reads my book, let him pass judgment on me. If I have said something reasonable, let him follow, not me, but reason itself; if I've proved it by the clearest divine testimony, let him follow, not me, but the divine scripture … I get angrier with that kind of fan of mine who takes my book as being canonical, than with the man who finds fault in my book with things that are not in fact at fault."[3]

There may be a touch of false humility in Augustine's suggestion to his readers but his message is clear: the response to his work was less important for Christians than their response to the truth.

Regardless of what Augustine wrote, devotion was not an unusual response for texts that pre-modern readers appreciated. That we are now accustomed to influential texts being honored with criticism represents an important difference between readers today and readers in Augustine's time. Augustine was a well-known bishop and, in the decades following his death, widely regarded as a saint and a highly respected teacher. It is no surprise that people should honor his work.

One example of this is *Vita Augustini* ("Life of Augustine"), written in 430, 30 years after Augustine's death by his friend Possidius.* Possidius only mentions *Confessions* twice.[4] *Vita Augustini* seems intended as a hagiography*—a text about the deeds of a saint. It was intended to honor Augustine rather than to report the full story of his life and work.

Conflict and Consensus

The reasons for Augustine's popularity and authority after his death are fairly self-evident. Augustine's education and his role as a Church leader prepared him to unite philosophy and everyday Church life in his teaching. In addition, more than anybody before him, Augustine wrote extensively in Latin, and he confronted questions and controversies that were important to the Church. Doing so established his reputation as a skilled and authoritative defender of Catholicism.*[5]

For example, Augustine played a particularly important role in the controversy caused by Pelagius,* a fifth-century theologian who taught that people could lead sinless lives and so, to some extent, they could earn salvation (a doctrine that became known as Pelagianism).* But Augustine argued that Pelagius's emphasis on a sinless life was incompatible with humans' reliance on God's grace—his affect on everyday human action. As a result of his opposition to Pelagius, Augustine earned a reputation as a polemical defender of Catholicism.[6]

His legacy endures; he is still remembered, and his works are still read for these contributions.

NOTES

1   Augustine, *Retractiones*, 2.6.33, in *Revisions*, ed. John Rotelle (New York: New City Press, 2010)

2   Augustine, *Letters,* ed. John Rotelle (New York: New City Press, 2002), 231.

3   Augustine, "Dolbeau 10," in *Sermons*, ed. John Rotelle, trans. Edmund Hill (New York: New City Press, 1997), 1:176–7.

4   Roy J. Deferrari, preface to "The Life of St. Augustine," by Possidius, in *Early Christian Biographies,* ed. Roy J. Deferrari (Washington: Catholic University Press, 1954).

5   Adam Ployd, *Augustine, the Trinity, and the Church: A Reading of the Anti-Donatist Sermons* (Oxford: Oxford University Press, 2015), 11.

6   Goulven Madec, "Augustinianism," in André Vauchez, ed. *Encyclopedia of the Middle Ages* (Chicago: James Clarke and Co, 2000), 1:132–3.

MODULE 10
THE EVOLVING DEBATE

KEY POINTS

- Augustine's choice of narrative is likely the most powerfully influential feature of *Confessions*.
- A number of disciplines that consider the sources of Western thinking—including theology, philosophy, and history—draw on *Confessions*.
- Today Roman Catholic theologians, Protestant theologians, and religious philosophers all study Augustine's *Confessions.*

Uses and Problems

While it is certain that Augustine's *Confessions* has influenced a number of academic disciplines, it is difficult to distinguish the specific ways that each has been shaped. It is perhaps more accurate to say that, like other pre-modern texts, it has shaped Western culture as a whole, and Western culture has, in turn, shaped various academic fields.

The easiest way to trace the book's theological influence is by examining which texts have looked to *Confessions* for insight. For example, if we see the text as a philosophical and theological account of Augustine's pilgrimage, then we might place it in the company of texts such as *The Consolation of Philosophy,* by the sixth-century Roman philosopher and statesman Boethius;* *Monologion* (1077) and *Proslogion* (1078), by the Benedictine monk and Archbishop of Canterbury Anselm;* *The Divine Comedy* (1472), an extraordinarily important work by the Italian poet Dante Alighieri;* and the English poet Geoffrey Chaucer's* *Canterbury Tales* (1475).

An equally respected tradition in which we could place *Confessions* includes Bonaventure,* a Franciscan friar known for his theological

❝ What do I love when I love my God? ❞

Augustine, *Confessions*

and philosophical works; the medieval Dominican priest Thomas Aquinas,* who heavily influenced philosophers and theologians; the sixteenth-century German monk Martin Luther,* whose *95 Theses* effectively began the Reformation,* a religious schism that saw the founding of the Protestant Church after a split with the Catholic branch of Christianity; and Friedrich Schleiermacher,* a German theologian and the father of modern systematic theology* (a way of studying Christian doctrines that draws on philosophy to explain the relationship between God and humanity).[1] This line of evolution can be traced to such topics as free will (the Christian doctrine that God deliberately gave mankind the choice of whether to sin or not, without which action cannot be judged), the relationship between philosophy and theology, moral theology, and Christology* (the study of the person and work of Jesus Christ).*

Most importantly, *Confessions* offered a new and influential vision for Christian theology. For example, while conversion was important before *Confessions,* it was rarely, if ever, the subject of theological reflection. Furthermore, it showed that Christology, Scripture, philosophy, and one's life story can be blended together to make an argument about spirituality. While *Confessions* is not systematic theology in the traditional sense, it is nonetheless a model for how various aspects of a person's life might come together in Christian thought.

Schools of Thought

Today, Augustine is typically read in undergraduate courses in which great works are studied, as well as by theologians, historians, and philosophers of religion. But while this might suggest that its readership is limited, readers today should be aware of its huge impact on important writers and scholars throughout history.

Thinkers as diverse as Boethius, Anselm, Aquinas, Geoffrey Chaucer, the French philosopher René Descartes,* and the Swiss philosopher and political theorist Jean-Jacques Rousseau* have been attracted by Augustine's masterpiece.

These thinkers are united in their interest in texts that have greatly informed Western theological or philosophical tradition, and their work shows that *Confessions* is still worth exploring. For example, some, like Anselm and Descartes, have adopted Augustine's first-person "voice"—the inquisitive *I*—for their own theological or philosophical projects.[2]

Others, such as Rousseau, Boethius, Aquinas, Schleiermacher, and Swiss theologian and Protestant reformer Karl Barth,* have chosen instead to critique, modify, or extend specific doctrinal or philosophical points that Augustine makes. That Augustine's work still inspires discussion and argument affirms its value not just as an historical text, but as an intellectually important one.

In Current Scholarship

While many groups of Christians claim Augustinian heritage, the author of *Confessions* has historically been associated with Roman Catholicism. In fact, a major collection of articles published by Roman Catholic Church historians in 1990 declared Augustine to be the "Second Founder of the Faith."[3]

But the community of Augustine scholars includes other groups, too. Some Protestant theologians have been attracted by Augustine's personal account because of its moral, Christological, biblical, and theological aspects.[4] There has also been lively interest from philosophers of religion, who have traditionally been attracted by Augustine's account of faith and reason, rationality and the passions, his interpretations of Scripture, and the problem of evil* (or how evil can exist at the same time as an all-powerful God).

It is telling that so many groups are interested in the text for different reasons. *Confessions* is a complex text that does not take a definite stance on a number of issues—meaning it has become the subject of considerable reinterpretation.

NOTES

1   All these influences, with specific textual evidence, can be found in Karla Pollman et al., eds., *The Oxford Guide to the Historical Reception of Augustine*, 3 vols. (Oxford: Oxford University Press, 2013).

2   See Anselm, *Monologion and Proslogion: With the replies of Gaunilo and Anselm*, trans. Thomas Williams (Indianapolis: Hackett, 1995); and René Descartes, *Discourse on Method and Meditations on First Philosophy*, 4th ed., trans. Donald A. Cress (Indianapolis: Hackett, 1998).

3   Joseph C. Schnaubelt, ed. *Collectanea Augustiniana: Augustine: "Second Founder of the Faith"* (Bern: Peter Lang, 1990).

4   Adolf von Harnack, "Augustins Confessionen," in Reden und Aufsätze (Verlag: Edition Cicero, 2002).

MODULE 11
IMPACT AND INFLUENCE TODAY

KEY POINTS

- Today, Augustine's *Confessions* stands as a landmark in the Western literary canon. It is appreciated for its language, psychological insight, and philosophical and theological originality.
- *Confessions* still challenges our ideas of subjectivity and authority.
- *Confessions* still provokes debate, especially about such issues as the relationship between faith and reason, and the role of human desire.

Position

About a century after Augustine's *Confessions* was published, the sixth-century Roman philosopher Boethius* showed his appreciation for the work in his own literary masterpiece. Although Boethius's *De consolatione philosophiae* ("The Consolations of Philosophy") is different in form, content, and tone, Augustine's *Confessions* was a major inspiration.

Boethius was not alone. While *Confessions* was not widely read in the Middle Ages, it experienced a revival during the late medieval period through the period of European cultural history known as the Renaissance,* in the course of which European culture was reinvigorated by a turn toward ancient Roman and Greek models in the arts and architecture. Many authors employed the same sort of personal narrative that Augustine did to help support a theological or philosophical argument. Some of these include the Italian poet Dante Alighieri,* the author of *The Divine Comedy* (1472), Desiderius

❝ But you, the Good, in need of no other good, are ever at rest since you yourself are your own rest. What man can enable the human mind to understand this? Which angel can interpret it to an angel? What angel can help a human being to grasp it? Only you can be asked, only you can be begged, only on your door can we knock. Yes indeed, that is how it is received, how it is found, how the door is opened. ❞

Augustine, final words of *Confessions*

Erasmus,* a Catholic priest who contributed significantly to humanist* thought (which emphasizes the knowledge and achievement of human beings over that of the divine), the Protestant* reformer Martin Luther,* and John Calvin,* a Protestant pastor and the father of the Christian sect of Calvinism.

Augustine continued to be influential during the early Enlightenment,* a major Western cultural and intellectual movement from the seventeenth to nineteenth centuries that produced revolutionary ideas about authority, reason, and individuality. The French philosopher René Descartes* borrowed Augustine's famous "I" in his *Meditations on First Philosophy*, and the Swiss writer and philosopher Jean-Jacques Rousseau* even gave Augustine the compliment of publishing his own work titled *Confessions*.

Augustine's *Confessions* became only more important as time passed, especially in the eyes of twentieth-century French and German scholars.[1] Comparisons were made not only with Descartes and Rousseau, but also with the eighteenth and nineteenth-century German poet and playwright Goethe's* most famous work *Faustus,* and with the psychologist Sigmund Freud's* pioneering work on memory.[2]

Interaction

In the late twentieth century, theology became a more self-conscious enterprise, in part because of the German philosopher Martin Heidegger's* work on being and existence, which has significantly influenced contemporary philosophers of religion. During this time, theologians began to consider more seriously how their prejudices affected their thinking and writing.

This turn to a greater awareness of subjectivity—the understanding that human perception plays a significant role in interpretation, with consequences for our various definitions of "truth"—paved the way for Augustine to become, once again, a theological model. Though Augustine's work did not speak to all the concerns of those who draw on postmodernism* (a philosophical perspective emphasizing how each person's experience is relative and considering how actions are influenced by powerful social forces), he has often been regarded as a champion of subjectivity.[3]

Augustine believed his view of the world had been formed by his past. This was directly opposed to Descartes's idea of the "naked ego" and to the German philosopher Immanuel Kant's* "objective investigator," both of which had to do with how people could examine their lives objectively.[4] Augustine presented his experience and his sins with an almost postmodern "authenticity"*—that is, he believed that the experience of the individual subject was important. This is not to say that Augustine himself was a postmodernist; his reverence for the Catholic Church, for example, is at cross-purposes with many postmodern goals.

That said, *Confessions* engages with the tension between individuality and authority in ways that may help readers strike a balance, both with theological hermeneutics,* or interpretation, and also critiques of power. For Augustine, personal authenticity and humble submission to God are inseparable.

The Continuing Debate

Several schools of theological thought continue to challenge *Confessions.* For example, while Augustine emphasized the importance of the Church in theological understanding, Protestant theologians argue that the Holy Spirit is more important than the Church.[5]

Another example is Augustine's account of faith and reason, which understands faith as seeking understanding. Analytic philosophers (those philosophers who value well-reasoned and supported arguments) of religion tend sometimes to argue that Augustine's account lacks common sense, since most people see faith and reason as directly opposed. They prefer writing that is explanatory or descriptive, as opposed to Augustine's narrative mode.[6]

Lastly, liberal theologians disagree with Augustine's description of human desire; some argue that Augustine introduces an unnecessary and dangerous opposition in which giving in to one's desires is bad and denying them is good, and others reinterpret *Confessions* to show that Augustine is not as unyielding on pursuing physical desire as has been thought.[7]

Many of these responses are based not simply on the intention of criticizing *Confessions.*   Augustine's importance to Christian thinking—and Western thought in general— means thatthere is political capital to be gained by toppling his position (or sustaining it, for that matter). He has been so central to Western theology, his ideas must be repeatedly confronted, and because *Confessions* is his most popular text, it is often the territory in which these confrontations occur.

NOTES

1   Adolf von Harnack, "Augustins Confessionen," in *Reden und Aufsätze* (Verlag: Edition Cicero, 2002); Pierre Courcelle, *Recherches sur les Confessions de Saint Augustin* (Paris: Boccard, 1950).

2   Harnack, "Augustin's Confessionen."

3   Catherine Malabou, "The Form of an 'I'," in *Augustine and Postmodernism: Confessions and Circumfession*, ed. John D. Caputo and Michael J. Scanlon (Bloomington, IN: Indiana University Press, 2005), 127–37.

4   See René Descartes, "Second Meditation: The nature of the human mind, and how it is better known than the body," in *Meditations on First Philosophy*, ed. John Cottingham (Cambridge: Cambridge University Press, 1996); Immanuel Kant, *Critique of Pure Reason*, (Cambridge: Cambridge University Press, 1998), B162.

5   Lewis Ayres, "Into the Poem of the Universe: Exempla, Conversion, and Church in Augustine's Confessiones," *Zeitschrift für antikes Christentum* (*Journal of Ancient Christianity*) 13, no: 2 (2009), 263–81.

6   John Rist, "Faith and Reason," in *The Cambridge Companion to Augustine*, ed. Eleonore Stump and Norman Kretzmann (Cambridge: Cambridge University Press, 2001), 26–39.

7   Charles Mathewes, *The Republic of Grace: Augustinian Thoughts for Dark Times* (Grand Rapids, MI: Eerdmans Press, 2010).

MODULE 12
WHERE NEXT?

KEY POINTS

- Augustine's *Confessions* is likely to remain a touchstone for reflections on the inner life and personality of the human being.

- *Confessions* still has its disciples today, including some who hold very important positions.

- Because of the beauty of its prose, its insights on human desires and failures, and the influence it has had on the Western literary canon, it is likely that the popularity and relevance of *Confessions* will endure.

Potential

Augustine's *Confessions* has remained relevant through the many social and cultural revolutions of Western society. The twentieth century was difficult for the study of religion and theology: theologians turned to new modes of study, and the academic world became more secular and oriented toward science. But lately, a renewed interest in religion—partly as a result of religious violence—has kept *Confessions* relevant for anyone interested in the European Christian traditions.

Theologians in particular seem interested in Augustine's mode of inquiry. Augustine's use of self-reflection spoke to both congregations and intellectuals, and contemporary authors wonder if they can use the same self-reflective techniques to engage complex and sophisticated concepts.

Many people also see value in Augustine's discussion of his desires, the way he reconciles individual wisdom with submission to authority, and how he discusses knowledge of the self as informed by theology.

66 And men go abroad to admire the heights of
mountains, the mighty waves of the sea, the broad tides
of rivers, the compass of the ocean, and the circuits
of the stars, yet pass over the mystery of themselves
without a thought. 99

Augustine, *Confessions*

Especially the last of these—theologically informed self-knowledge—
has caught on, as it brings theology into a critical dialogue with today's
research in philosophy of mind (inquiry into philosophical
considerations of consciousness and identity), neuroscience (the study
of the function and nature of the brain and nervous system) and
sociopsychological development (the role of human psychology in
social behavior).[1]

Scholars will continue to take up the core ideas of *Confessions*. The
promise of further development seems also to reside in thinkers who
are interested in interdisciplinary projects (that is, projects that draw
on the aims and methods of different academic fields), particularly
those that take seriously the historical formation of contemporary
mindsets and institutions.

Future Directions

There have been many Augustinian historians in the centuries since
his death, and today is no exception. Among those who engage with
his thoughts are Emeritus Pope Benedict XVI (Joseph Ratzinger),*
former Archbishop of Canterbury Rowan Williams,* the influential
philosopher of ethics Alasdair MacIntyre,* and the French philosopher
Jean-Luc Marion.*[2]

Pope Benedict and former Archbishop Williams represent Roman
Catholic and Anglican traditions respectively. Benedict wrote his

dissertation on Augustinian ecclesiology (the study of the Church's history and theology); in particular, he defended Augustine's conception of the Church as both the *people* of God and the *house* of God.[3] Former Archbishop Williams has highlighted Augustine's spirituality. He focuses on how Augustine is able to successfully combine a rigorous understanding of God's action with the rich inner life of Christian existence.

For both these thinkers, *Confessions* has served as an important source text, useful for discussions both in and out of a Church context. Benedict and Williams's work hold promise for dialogues beyond the influence of the churches they led.

Others who have been perhaps less visible than Benedict and Williams have also drawn on Augustine. Jean-Luc Marion and Alasdair MacIntyre, for instance, act as Augustine's modern disciples in philosophical circles. Marion championed Augustine's concept of subjectivity and his religiously-informed phenomenology* (a type of philosophy that studies consciousness and perception). MacIntyre, a professor at the University of Notre Dame, has studied Augustine's use of narrative, focusing especially on what the text reveals about morality and epistemology* (the study of how knowledge is made).

While *Confessions* addresses neither subjectivity nor narrative directly, readers today can see how these modern concepts shape Augustine's text. In this way, Marion and MacIntyre both draw on and modernize *Confessions*, granting it a newfound relevance to contemporary philosophy.

Summary

During the Enlightenment,* the German philosopher Immanuel Kant* said: "Two things fill the mind with ever-increasing wonder and awe, the more often and the more intensely the mind of thought is drawn to them: the starry heavens above me and the moral law within me."[4] While science has provided a sense of wonder at the distant heavens above, *Confessions* reminds us of the wonder of our inner landscapes—that which is closest to us, and yet perhaps just as difficult to understand.

Confessions provides us with a model—the pilgrim saint—of our selves: it encourages us to see being as a process of change, flux, and development. Augustine's account has changed the way we write and talk about ourselves.

As history suggests, *Confessions* is likely to continue coming in and out of favor. After the renewed interest of the late nineteenth and twentieth centuries, scholarship on *Confessions* is currently in bloom: contemporary discussions of theology and religion focus on what it can tell us about subjectivity (the understanding that our identity and expectations alter our interpretation of what we experience) and narrative. Indeed, there is no reason to believe that after 1600 years, Western readers are losing interest.

The enduring status of *Confessions* comes, perhaps more than anything, from its poetic prose. The interior register of Augustine's texts—Augustine's inner voice—continues to delight and engage scholars and general readers alike. Augustine's *Confessions* provides a picture of the human that is at once ancient and new, and that delights as much as it informs its reader.

NOTES

1   William E. Mann, "The Life of the Mind in Dramas and Dreams," in William E. Mann, ed. *Augustine's Confessions: Philosophy in Autobiography* (Oxford: Oxford University Press, 2014), 108–34.

2   See Joseph Ratzinger, *'In the Beginning…': A Catholic Understanding of the Story of Creation and the Fall* (Grand Rapids, MI: Eerdmans, 1995); Rowan Williams, *The Edge of Words: God and the Habits of Language* (London: Bloomsbury, 2014); Alasdair MacIntyre, *God, Philosophy, Universities: A Selective History of the Catholic Philosophical Tradition* (Notre Dame: University of Notre Dame Press, 2011); and Jean-Luc Marion, *In the Self's Place: The Approach of Saint Augustine*, trans. Jeffrey L. Kosky (Stanford, CA: Stanford University Press, 2012).

3   Aidan Nichols, *The Theology of Joseph Ratzinger: An Introductory Study* (Edinburgh: T&T Clark, 1988), 33.

4   Immanuel Kant, *Practical Philosophy* (Cambridge: Cambridge University Press, 1999), 269.

GLOSSARY

GLOSSARY OF TERMS

Academicians: sometimes referred to as members of the "New Academy," the Academicians came together under the Greek philosopher Arcesilaus's distaste for the methods of Plato's early works in the third century B.C.E. Under its most influential head, Carneades, Academicians gained the status of skeptics. While the school itself fell apart in doctrinal disarray in the first century B.C.E., a group of philosophers in the fourth century C.E. revived the skepticism of the Academicians through the influence of the Roman orator and philosopher Cicero's writings.

Ascent: the soul's journey toward God. This is one of several important concepts described in Augustine's *Confessions.*

Asceticism: the practice of training to give the soul control over the body and its desires. While ascetical techniques and strategies were adopted by monastic orders, in the fourth century it was possible to call oneself an ascetic while married or living outside a formal community of monks.

Authenticity: the philosophical claim, often associated with the influential philosopher Jean-Paul Sartre (1905–80), that people should be true to their own personalities, spirits, or characters despite external pressures not to. This has become an influential belief system in Western countries.

Beatific vision: the immediate knowledge of God enjoyed by those in the presence of God. It is called "vision" to distinguish it from more distant ways of knowing God, such as through reason or authority. The beatific vision, to Augustine, occurs only in the next life, but there are certain hints in this one.

Catholicism: a term that, in the fourth century, referred to Nicene Christians. Catholics made up the largest sect, and smaller sects often sought to define theological positions against them. At this time, Catholicism extended to both the Greek and Latin Churches, even though differences were already beginning to appear between them.

Christology: study of the person and work of Jesus Christ.

Deconstructionism: a concept derived from the critical theory associated with the philosopher Jacques Derrida's foundational text *Of Grammatology* (1967), which first appeared in English translation in 1976 and has been influential in Western thought ever since. It assumes that differences between things are largely, if not wholly, linguistically constructed.

Donatism: a form of Christianity practiced in fourth-century North Africa. The Donatist sect became the target of many polemical writings by Augustine because its members believed that their own practices constituted the only valid form of Christianity.

Enlightenment: a major Western cultural and intellectual movement between the late seventeenth and early nineteenth centuries. Enlightenment thinkers reacted against traditional authority, especially the church, and emphasized reason, analysis, and individualism.

Epistemology: study of the method or grounds for knowledge.

Eudaemonia: roughly, an ancient philosophical word for happiness describing how much a person has used his or her talents and enjoyed him or herself over the entirety of their life.

Hagiography: writing about deeds and actions of holy men or women, especially saints; hagiography was especially prominent in

Christian literature from 400 to 1600 C.E.

Hermeneutics: a branch of philosophy that deals with interpretation.

Humanism: a cultural and philosophical world view that emerged in the Renaissance of the fourteenth to sixteenth centuries. Humanism emphasizes the possibilities of human knowledge and achievement (rather than divine or supernatural explanations). Humanist thought assumes that human beings are fundamentally good, values self-definition, and seeks rational solution to problems.

Immateriality: the quality of being non-material, or of not being made of matter. Also referred to as "incorporeal."

Incarnation: a process of something immaterial becoming flesh. In the Christian tradition, the word commonly refers to the belief that God became human in the person of Jesus Christ of Nazareth.

Jesus Christ: central figure of the Christian religion. The historical person of Jesus Christ conducted a mission of preaching and healing in Palestine around 28–30 C.E., and was believed to be the Son of God by his followers.

Manichaeans: sect founded by Mani, a third-century Mesopotamian religious leader. Manichaeans believed that the world was created entirely from preexisting matter, and that some of that matter was "good" and some "evil." Thus, they often adopted strict physical constraints, such as celibacy, a vegetarian diet, and foregoing alcohol. Manichaeans had great respect for the Apostle Paul and disregarded the Old Testament and much of the Gospel narratives. The Manichaean sect eventually disappeared from the Mediterranean world, and is now known chiefly through Augustine's texts.

Materialism: the theory or belief that nothing exists except matter and its movements and modifications. It also describes the modern belief that mental phenomena are caused by material or physical forces.

Metaphysics: branch of philosophy that deals with the first principles of things, including being, knowledge, causes, time, and space.

Neoplatonism: type of Platonist philosophy begun by the Greek philosopher Plotinus based on the belief that the soul was engaged in a mystical quest toward union with God. This philosophy influenced Augustine's understanding of the soul's journey to God.

Nicene Christianity: the Christian traditions that came about as a result of theological disputes in the fourth and fifth centuries. In general, pro-Nicene Christians declared that Jesus was the Son of God and the second member of the Trinity, and the Holy Spirit as the third member of Trinity. Nicene Christianity also affirmed the authority of bishops.

Non-materialism: a type of philosophy that is opposed to materialism; it is common among Platonist philosophers.

Pelagianism: a Christian heresy named after the fifth-century Christian theologian Pelagius, who argued that people could live just and righteous lives. In some parts of the world, this belief would not have been controversial; however the North African church was committed to idea that God affected all human actions. Pelagianism's most fearsome opponent was Augustine, who spent the final 20 years of his life combating what he perceived to be the denial of the importance of God's grace in Christians' lives.

Phenomenology: a school of philosophy that focuses on the immediate perception of things, events, and others. Founded by Edmund Husserl, an early twentieth-century German philosopher, its influential advocates included Martin Heidegger, Maurice Merleau-Ponty, and Jean-Paul Sartre.

Platonism: the philosophical schools that adhere to the teachings of the Greek philosopher Plato (428–347 B.C.E.), often considered the father of Western philosophy. Platonism offered an influential concept of the pursuit of wisdom, which Augustine both confronts and critiques in *Confessions.* In the fourth century C.E., Platonism was further developed by the writings of the philosopher Plotinus (c. 204–70) and his pupil Pophyry (234–305), who incorporated the ideas of many other late antique philosophies into Platonism.

Postmodernism: a set of scholarly and artistic concerns and methods that emerged in the second half of the twentieth century. Postmodern philosophy emphasizes subjectivity and relativity, and investigates the power relationships that influence one's thoughts and beliefs.

Problem of evil: the modern name for the question of why evil is permitted by a supreme being or God.

Reformation: a split in the European Christian community of the sixteenth century provoked by the German minister Martin Luther and others, which saw the foundation of the Protestant Church.

Renaissance: a period of European cultural history, commonly defined as the mid-fourteenth century to the sixteenth century, in which cultural forms (especially art, music, and literature) were reinvigorated by a turn toward classic models.

Rhetoric: the study and methods of the use of language to inform, persuade, and motivate one's audience.

Schools of wisdom: formed during the Roman Empire to teach followers both a philosophy and a way of life. Joining a school of wisdom usually involved a commitment to ascetic practice.

Systematic theology: the study of Christian doctrines, their sources, and how they relate. Often drawing on philosophical models, systematic theology seeks to make Christian doctrine a coherent set of principles that explain God, humanity, and their relationship.

Theologist: one engaged in the systematic study of religious concepts—God, the nature of heaven, the divine status of Jesus Christ, for example—commonly using scripture.

PEOPLE MENTIONED IN THE TEXT

Adeodatus (372–390) was Augustine's son, mothered by Augustine's concubine, and baptized by Ambrose with Augustine in 387. In 390, Adeodatus died, causing his father much grief. It is generally believed that Adeodatus was exceptionally intelligent, evidence of which can be seen in Augustine's final dialogue, *De magistro* ("On the Teacher," 389).

Ambrose of Milan (c. 330–97) was bishop of Milan from 374 until his death. He is known as a powerful anti-Arian bishop, a defender of asceticism and celibacy, and a major influence on Augustine. Ambrose demonstrated that the Old Testament could be read with more nuance than was typical in North African churches.

Anselm of Canterbury (1033–1109) was a Benedictine monk and philosopher who served as archbishop of Canterbury from 1093 until his death. He is best known for his theological and philosophical works.

Thomas Aquinas (1225–74) was a Dominican priest known for his philosophical and theological works. He is one of the most influential theologians to write in Latin, and is widely read in both philosophy and theology today.

Karl Barth (1886–1968) was an important Swiss Protestant theologian. He reacted strongly to liberal theology and its political influences, and sought to build a systematic theology more focused on the revelation of the Word in the person of Jesus Christ.

Boethius (480–524) was a philosopher and statesman in early sixth century Rome. He is mostly remembered today for the *Consolation of Philosophy*, which he wrote while imprisoned and awaiting execution.

Bonaventure (1221–74) was a Franciscan friar known for his theological and philosophical works. His best-known work *Itinerarium Mentis in Deum* ("Journey of the Mind to God") is generally regarded as addressing the Augustinian question of the Christian soul's ascent to God.

John Calvin (1509–64) was a French theologian and pastor during the Protestant Reformation. He is known for his *Institutes of the Christian Religion*, which used Renaissance humanist principles to interpret Christian scriptures and doctrine.

Geoffrey Chaucer (1343–1400) was an English poet and one of the most important figures in the tradition of English literature. His best-known work, *Canterbury Tales,* is a collection of stories told by pilgrims on their way to Canterbury.

Marcus Tullius Cicero (106–43 B.C.E.) was a Roman philosopher, politician, lawyer, orator, political theorist, consul, and constitutionalist.

Dante Alighieri (1265–1321) was a Florentine poet and politician best known for his *Commedia* (*The Divine Comedy*), often considered the most important poem written in Italian. It is still read by every young person in Italy today. Some scholars have argued that *Commedia* draws its model of pilgrimage from Augustine.

Rene Descartes (1596–1650) was a French philosopher who pioneered the field of epistemology. Central to his philosophy was the idea of the "naked ego"—a stripping away of historical and social context in order to come to a belief that one could know with absolute certainty.

Desiderius Erasmus (1466–1536), known as Erasmus of Rotterdam, was a Dutch Renaissance humanist and Catholic priest.

He is known for his remarkable breadth of knowledge, his contributions to Renaissance humanism, and his argumentative writings about the Protestant Reformation.

Sigmund Freud (1856–1939) is known as the father of psychoanalysis. He spent the majority of his career in Vienna, Austria, working as a writer and a practicing psychoanalyst. He is celebrated for his concept of the unconscious and the role it plays in our actions and thinking.

Johann Wolfgang von Goethe (1749–1832) was a German writer and statesman. Most famous for the drama *Faust*, he left behind many works of fiction and criticism. Today, he is one of the most widely read German authors.

Martin Heidegger (1889–1976) was a German philosopher whose work has powerfully influenced twentieth-century philosophy. Heidegger explored questions of being and existence and argued that interpretation was important for understanding what happens in the world.

Immanuel Kant (1724–1804) was a German philosopher whose ideas were foundational to Enlightenment philosophy and continue to be relevant today. Kant's "objective investigator" describes the unbiased stance that he believed would ensure objectivity.

Martin Luther (1483–1546) was a German monk in the Augustinian order and a professor of theology. On October 31, 1517, he published his *95 Theses* against the practice of indulgences in the Catholic Church. He is thus known as the father of the Protestant Reformation and of "Lutheranism," a sect prominent in Germany, Sweden, and the United States.

Alasdair MacIntyre (b. 1929) is a Scottish philosopher who has spent the majority of his career in the United States. He is best known for his work of moral philosophy, *After Virtue* (1981).

Jean-Luc Marion (b. 1946) is a French philosopher who teaches at the University of Chicago and the University of Paris IV–Sorbonne. He is also a member of the Academie française, the most distinguished honor in the French academy.

Monica was Augustine's mother and a devout Catholic Christian. Today, she is revered as a saint for supporting Augustine's faith early in his life.

Paul the Apostle (c. 5 B.C.E.–c. 62-4 C.E.) was the author of several New Testament epistles (letters). His work greatly influenced Augustine (especially in the years before Augustine wrote *Confessions*). Augustine develops his understanding of grace from Paul's writings in the New Testament books of Romans and Galatians.

Plato (428–347 B.C.E.) is often considered the father of Western philosophy. He is known for *The Republic, Symposium, Apology,* and *Phaedrus.*

Plotinus (204/5–270 C.E.) was a Greek philosopher who lived and taught in Alexandria and Rome. He was known during his day as a teacher of philosophy. The *Enneads*, which were later edited by his student Porphyry, are an influential work in the Alexandrian school of late Platonic thought.

Porphyry (c. 232–305 C.E.) was a Greek philosopher and critic of Christianity. He is known for editing Plotinus's *Enneads* and for his brief biography of Plotinus. In his own work, he applied

Neoplatonism (a style of Platonist philosophy introduced by Plotinus) to pagan religious thought.

Possidius (late fourth–fifth century C.E.) was a friend and biographer of Augustine's.

Joseph Ratzinger (b. 1927) served as head of the Roman Catholic Church as Pope Benedict XVI from 2005 until his resignation in 2013. As an academic, Ratzinger wrote about Augustine, Bonaventure, and Catholic theology.

Jean-Jacques Rousseau (1712–78) was a philosopher, writer, and composer from Geneva in Switzerland. His political philosophy was a major influence in the French Enlightenment during the eighteenth century.

Friedrich Schleiermacher (1768–1834) was a German theologian, philosopher, and biblical scholar. He is generally regarded as the father of modern systematic theology.

Adolf von Harnack (1851–1930) was a German church historian and theologian of the Protestant Lutheran sect. He is often considered the father of the academic study of church history. His *History of Dogma* and *What Is Christianity?* are still major source texts in the field of historical theology.

Rowan Williams (b. 1950) is the former Archbishop of Canterbury and leader of the worldwide Anglican community. He is known for his works on the history of Christian spirituality, theology, and poetry.

WORKS CITED

WORKS CITED

Alfaric, Prosper. *L'Évolution intellectuelle de Saint Augustin* (Paris: Emile Nourry, 1918).

Ayres, Lewis. *Nicaea and its Legacy: An Approach to Fourth-Century Trinitarian Theology.* Oxford: University of Oxford Press, 2004.

Bonner, Gerald. *St Augustine of Hippo: Life and Controversies.* Third edition. Norwich: Canterbury Press, 2002.

Courcelle, Pierre. *Recherches sur les Confessions de Saint Augustin:* Nouvelle édition augmentée et illustrée. Paris: Éditions E. de Boccard, 1968.

Flasch, Kurth. *Augustin: Einführung in Sein Denken.* Stuttgart: Reclam, 1980.

Lancel, Serge. *St Augustine.* Translated by Antonia Nevill. London: SCM Press, 2002.

Lettieri, Gaetano. *L'altro Agostino. Ermeneutica e Retorica Della Grazia Dalla Crisi Alla Metamorfosi Del De Doctrina Christiana.* Brescia: Morcelliana, 2002.

Lorenz, Rudolf. "Augustin." In *Religion in Geschichte Und Gegenwart.* Tübingen: Mohr Siebeck, 1957.

MacIntyre, Alasdair. *Three Rival Versions of Moral Enquiry: Encyclopaedia, Genealogy and Tradition.* Revised edition. Notre Dame, IN: University of Notre Dame Press, 1992.

Madec, G. S. *Saint Augustin et la Philosophie.* Paris: Études Augustiniennes, 1996.

Marion, Jean-Luc. *In the Self's Place: The Approach of Saint Augustine.* Translated by Jeffrey L. Kosky. Stanford, CA: Stanford University Press, 2012.

Nichols, Aidan. *The Theology of Joseph Ratzinger: An Introductory Study.* Edinburgh: T&T Clark, 1988.

O'Connell, Robert J. *St. Augustine's Confessions: The Odyssey of Soul.* Cambridge, MA: Belknap Harvard University Press, 1969.

O'Donnell, James J. *Augustine Confessions. Vol. I: Introduction and Text.* Oxford: Oxford University Press, 1992.

———. *Augustine, Sinner and Saint: A New Biography.* London: Profile Books Ltd, 2005.

Possidius. *Life of Saint Augustine.* Translated by Herbert T. Weiskotten. Princeton: Princeton University Press, 1919.

Ratzinger, Joseph. "Originalität und Überlieferung in Augustins Begriff der *confessio*," *Revue Des Études Augustiniennes et Patristiques* 3, no. 4 (1957): 375–92.

———. *Volk und Haus Gottes in Augustins Lehre von der Kirche.* München: Eos Verlag U. Druck, 1992.

Van Fleteren, Frederick. "Augustine's Ascent of the Soul in Book VII of the *Confessions*: A Reconsideration." *Augustinian Studies* 5 (1974): 29–72.

von Harnack, Adolf. "Augustins *Confessionen*," in *Reden Und Aufsätze.* Verlag: Edition Cicero, 2002.

Wetzel, James. *Augustine and the Limits of Virtue.* Cambridge: Cambridge University Press, 1992.

Williams, Rowan. *The Wound of Knowledge: Christian Spirituality from the New Testament to St. John of the Cross.* London: Darton, Longman and Todd, 1979.

THE MACAT LIBRARY
BY DISCIPLINE

AFRICANA STUDIES

Chinua Achebe's *An Image of Africa: Racism in Conrad's Heart of Darkness*
W. E. B. Du Bois's *The Souls of Black Folk*
Zora Neale Huston's *Characteristics of Negro Expression*
Martin Luther King Jr's *Why We Can't Wait*
Toni Morrison's *Playing in the Dark: Whiteness in the American Literary Imagination*

ANTHROPOLOGY

Arjun Appadurai's *Modernity at Large: Cultural Dimensions of Globalisation*
Philippe Ariès's *Centuries of Childhood*
Franz Boas's *Race, Language and Culture*
Kim Chan & Renée Mauborgne's *Blue Ocean Strategy*
Jared Diamond's *Guns, Germs & Steel: the Fate of Human Societies*
Jared Diamond's *Collapse: How Societies Choose to Fail or Survive*
E. E. Evans-Pritchard's *Witchcraft, Oracles and Magic Among the Azande*
James Ferguson's *The Anti-Politics Machine*
Clifford Geertz's *The Interpretation of Cultures*
David Graeber's *Debt: the First 5000 Years*
Karen Ho's *Liquidated: An Ethnography of Wall Street*
Geert Hofstede's *Culture's Consequences: Comparing Values, Behaviors, Institutes and Organizations across Nations*
Claude Lévi-Strauss's *Structural Anthropology*
Jay Macleod's *Ain't No Makin' It: Aspirations and Attainment in a Low-Income Neighborhood*
Saba Mahmood's *The Politics of Piety: The Islamic Revival and the Feminist Subject*
Marcel Mauss's *The Gift*

BUSINESS

Jean Lave & Etienne Wenger's *Situated Learning*
Theodore Levitt's *Marketing Myopia*
Burton G. Malkiel's *A Random Walk Down Wall Street*
Douglas McGregor's *The Human Side of Enterprise*
Michael Porter's *Competitive Strategy: Creating and Sustaining Superior Performance*
John Kotter's *Leading Change*
C. K. Prahalad & Gary Hamel's *The Core Competence of the Corporation*

CRIMINOLOGY

Michelle Alexander's *The New Jim Crow: Mass Incarceration in the Age of Colorblindness*
Michael R. Gottfredson & Travis Hirschi's *A General Theory of Crime*
Richard Herrnstein & Charles A. Murray's *The Bell Curve: Intelligence and Class Structure in American Life*
Elizabeth Loftus's *Eyewitness Testimony*
Jay Macleod's *Ain't No Makin' It: Aspirations and Attainment in a Low-Income Neighborhood*
Philip Zimbardo's *The Lucifer Effect*

ECONOMICS

Janet Abu-Lughod's *Before European Hegemony*
Ha-Joon Chang's *Kicking Away the Ladder*
David Brion Davis's *The Problem of Slavery in the Age of Revolution*
Milton Friedman's *The Role of Monetary Policy*
Milton Friedman's *Capitalism and Freedom*
David Graeber's *Debt: the First 5000 Years*
Friedrich Hayek's *The Road to Serfdom*
Karen Ho's *Liquidated: An Ethnography of Wall Street*

John Maynard Keynes's *The General Theory of Employment, Interest and Money*
Charles P. Kindleberger's *Manias, Panics and Crashes*
Robert Lucas's *Why Doesn't Capital Flow from Rich to Poor Countries?*
Burton G. Malkiel's *A Random Walk Down Wall Street*
Thomas Robert Malthus's *An Essay on the Principle of Population*
Karl Marx's *Capital*
Thomas Piketty's *Capital in the Twenty-First Century*
Amartya Sen's *Development as Freedom*
Adam Smith's *The Wealth of Nations*
Nassim Nicholas Taleb's *The Black Swan: The Impact of the Highly Improbable*
Amos Tversky's & Daniel Kahneman's *Judgment under Uncertainty: Heuristics and Biases*
Mahbub Ul Haq's *Reflections on Human Development*
Max Weber's *The Protestant Ethic and the Spirit of Capitalism*

FEMINISM AND GENDER STUDIES

Judith Butler's *Gender Trouble*
Simone De Beauvoir's *The Second Sex*
Michel Foucault's *History of Sexuality*
Betty Friedan's *The Feminine Mystique*
Saba Mahmood's *The Politics of Piety: The Islamic Revival and the Feminist Subject*
Joan Wallach Scott's *Gender and the Politics of History*
Mary Wollstonecraft's *A Vindication of the Rights of Woman*
Virginia Woolf's *A Room of One's Own*

GEOGRAPHY

The Brundtland Report's *Our Common Future*
Rachel Carson's *Silent Spring*
Charles Darwin's *On the Origin of Species*
James Ferguson's *The Anti-Politics Machine*
Jane Jacobs's *The Death and Life of Great American Cities*
James Lovelock's *Gaia: A New Look at Life on Earth*
Amartya Sen's *Development as Freedom*
Mathis Wackernagel & William Rees's *Our Ecological Footprint*

HISTORY

Janet Abu-Lughod's *Before European Hegemony*
Benedict Anderson's *Imagined Communities*
Bernard Bailyn's *The Ideological Origins of the American Revolution*
Hanna Batatu's *The Old Social Classes And The Revolutionary Movements Of Iraq*
Christopher Browning's *Ordinary Men: Reserve Police Batallion 101 and the Final Solution in Poland*
Edmund Burke's *Reflections on the Revolution in France*
William Cronon's *Nature's Metropolis: Chicago And The Great West*
Alfred W. Crosby's *The Columbian Exchange*
Hamid Dabashi's *Iran: A People Interrupted*
David Brion Davis's *The Problem of Slavery in the Age of Revolution*
Nathalie Zemon Davis's *The Return of Martin Guerre*
Jared Diamond's *Guns, Germs & Steel: the Fate of Human Societies*
Frank Dikotter's *Mao's Great Famine*
John W Dower's *War Without Mercy: Race And Power In The Pacific War*
W. E. B. Du Bois's *The Souls of Black Folk*
Richard J. Evans's *In Defence of History*
Lucien Febvre's *The Problem of Unbelief in the 16th Century*
Sheila Fitzpatrick's *Everyday Stalinism*

The Macat Library By Discipline

Eric Foner's *Reconstruction: America's Unfinished Revolution, 1863-1877*
Michel Foucault's *Discipline and Punish*
Michel Foucault's *History of Sexuality*
Francis Fukuyama's *The End of History and the Last Man*
John Lewis Gaddis's *We Now Know: Rethinking Cold War History*
Ernest Gellner's *Nations and Nationalism*
Eugene Genovese's *Roll, Jordan, Roll: The World the Slaves Made*
Carlo Ginzburg's *The Night Battles*
Daniel Goldhagen's *Hitler's Willing Executioners*
Jack Goldstone's *Revolution and Rebellion in the Early Modern World*
Antonio Gramsci's *The Prison Notebooks*
Alexander Hamilton, John Jay & James Madison's *The Federalist Papers*
Christopher Hill's *The World Turned Upside Down*
Carole Hillenbrand's *The Crusades: Islamic Perspectives*
Thomas Hobbes's *Leviathan*
Eric Hobsbawm's *The Age Of Revolution*
John A. Hobson's *Imperialism: A Study*
Albert Hourani's *History of the Arab Peoples*
Samuel P. Huntington's *The Clash of Civilizations and the Remaking of World Order*
C. L. R. James's *The Black Jacobins*
Tony Judt's *Postwar: A History of Europe Since 1945*
Ernst Kantorowicz's *The King's Two Bodies: A Study in Medieval Political Theology*
Paul Kennedy's *The Rise and Fall of the Great Powers*
Ian Kershaw's *The "Hitler Myth": Image and Reality in the Third Reich*
John Maynard Keynes's *The General Theory of Employment, Interest and Money*
Charles P. Kindleberger's *Manias, Panics and Crashes*
Martin Luther King Jr's *Why We Can't Wait*
Henry Kissinger's *World Order: Reflections on the Character of Nations and the Course of History*
Thomas Kuhn's *The Structure of Scientific Revolutions*
Georges Lefebvre's *The Coming of the French Revolution*
John Locke's *Two Treatises of Government*
Niccolò Machiavelli's *The Prince*
Thomas Robert Malthus's *An Essay on the Principle of Population*
Mahmood Mamdani's *Citizen and Subject: Contemporary Africa And The Legacy Of Late Colonialism*
Karl Marx's *Capital*
Stanley Milgram's *Obedience to Authority*
John Stuart Mill's *On Liberty*
Thomas Paine's *Common Sense*
Thomas Paine's *Rights of Man*
Geoffrey Parker's *Global Crisis: War, Climate Change and Catastrophe in the Seventeenth Century*
Jonathan Riley-Smith's *The First Crusade and the Idea of Crusading*
Jean-Jacques Rousseau's *The Social Contract*
Joan Wallach Scott's *Gender and the Politics of History*
Theda Skocpol's *States and Social Revolutions*
Adam Smith's *The Wealth of Nations*
Timothy Snyder's *Bloodlands: Europe Between Hitler and Stalin*
Sun Tzu's *The Art of War*
Keith Thomas's *Religion and the Decline of Magic*
Thucydides's *The History of the Peloponnesian War*
Frederick Jackson Turner's *The Significance of the Frontier in American History*
Odd Arne Westad's *The Global Cold War: Third World Interventions And The Making Of Our Times*

LITERATURE

Chinua Achebe's *An Image of Africa: Racism in Conrad's Heart of Darkness*
Roland Barthes's *Mythologies*
Homi K. Bhabha's *The Location of Culture*
Judith Butler's *Gender Trouble*
Simone De Beauvoir's *The Second Sex*
Ferdinand De Saussure's *Course in General Linguistics*
T. S. Eliot's *The Sacred Wood: Essays on Poetry and Criticism*
Zora Neale Huston's *Characteristics of Negro Expression*
Toni Morrison's *Playing in the Dark: Whiteness in the American Literary Imagination*
Edward Said's *Orientalism*
Gayatri Chakravorty Spivak's *Can the Subaltern Speak?*
Mary Wollstonecraft's *A Vindication of the Rights of Women*
Virginia Woolf's *A Room of One's Own*

PHILOSOPHY

Elizabeth Anscombe's *Modern Moral Philosophy*
Hannah Arendt's *The Human Condition*
Aristotle's *Metaphysics*
Aristotle's *Nicomachean Ethics*
Edmund Gettier's *Is Justified True Belief Knowledge?*
Georg Wilhelm Friedrich Hegel's *Phenomenology of Spirit*
David Hume's *Dialogues Concerning Natural Religion*
David Hume's *The Enquiry for Human Understanding*
Immanuel Kant's *Religion within the Boundaries of Mere Reason*
Immanuel Kant's *Critique of Pure Reason*
Søren Kierkegaard's *The Sickness Unto Death*
Søren Kierkegaard's *Fear and Trembling*
C. S. Lewis's *The Abolition of Man*
Alasdair MacIntyre's *After Virtue*
Marcus Aurelius's *Meditations*
Friedrich Nietzsche's *On the Genealogy of Morality*
Friedrich Nietzsche's *Beyond Good and Evil*
Plato's *Republic*
Plato's *Symposium*
Jean-Jacques Rousseau's *The Social Contract*
Gilbert Ryle's *The Concept of Mind*
Baruch Spinoza's *Ethics*
Sun Tzu's *The Art of War*
Ludwig Wittgenstein's *Philosophical Investigations*

POLITICS

Benedict Anderson's *Imagined Communities*
Aristotle's *Politics*
Bernard Bailyn's *The Ideological Origins of the American Revolution*
Edmund Burke's *Reflections on the Revolution in France*
John C. Calhoun's *A Disquisition on Government*
Ha-Joon Chang's *Kicking Away the Ladder*
Hamid Dabashi's *Iran: A People Interrupted*
Hamid Dabashi's *Theology of Discontent: The Ideological Foundation of the Islamic Revolution in Iran*
Robert Dahl's *Democracy and its Critics*
Robert Dahl's *Who Governs?*
David Brion Davis's *The Problem of Slavery in the Age of Revolution*

The Macat Library By Discipline

Alexis De Tocqueville's *Democracy in America*
James Ferguson's *The Anti-Politics Machine*
Frank Dikotter's *Mao's Great Famine*
Sheila Fitzpatrick's *Everyday Stalinism*
Eric Foner's *Reconstruction: America's Unfinished Revolution, 1863-1877*
Milton Friedman's *Capitalism and Freedom*
Francis Fukuyama's *The End of History and the Last Man*
John Lewis Gaddis's *We Now Know: Rethinking Cold War History*
Ernest Gellner's *Nations and Nationalism*
David Graeber's *Debt: the First 5000 Years*
Antonio Gramsci's *The Prison Notebooks*
Alexander Hamilton, John Jay & James Madison's *The Federalist Papers*
Friedrich Hayek's *The Road to Serfdom*
Christopher Hill's *The World Turned Upside Down*
Thomas Hobbes's *Leviathan*
John A. Hobson's *Imperialism: A Study*
Samuel P. Huntington's *The Clash of Civilizations and the Remaking of World Order*
Tony Judt's *Postwar: A History of Europe Since 1945*
David C. Kang's *China Rising: Peace, Power and Order in East Asia*
Paul Kennedy's *The Rise and Fall of Great Powers*
Robert Keohane's *After Hegemony*
Martin Luther King Jr.'s *Why We Can't Wait*
Henry Kissinger's *World Order: Reflections on the Character of Nations and the Course of History*
John Locke's *Two Treatises of Government*
Niccolò Machiavelli's *The Prince*
Thomas Robert Malthus's *An Essay on the Principle of Population*
Mahmood Mamdani's *Citizen and Subject: Contemporary Africa And The Legacy Of Late Colonialism*
Karl Marx's *Capital*
John Stuart Mill's *On Liberty*
John Stuart Mill's *Utilitarianism*
Hans Morgenthau's *Politics Among Nations*
Thomas Paine's *Common Sense*
Thomas Paine's *Rights of Man*
Thomas Piketty's *Capital in the Twenty-First Century*
Robert D. Putman's *Bowling Alone*
John Rawls's *Theory of Justice*
Jean-Jacques Rousseau's *The Social Contract*
Theda Skocpol's *States and Social Revolutions*
Adam Smith's *The Wealth of Nations*
Sun Tzu's *The Art of War*
Henry David Thoreau's *Civil Disobedience*
Thucydides's *The History of the Peloponnesian War*
Kenneth Waltz's *Theory of International Politics*
Max Weber's *Politics as a Vocation*
Odd Arne Westad's *The Global Cold War: Third World Interventions And The Making Of Our Times*

POSTCOLONIAL STUDIES

Roland Barthes's *Mythologies*
Frantz Fanon's *Black Skin, White Masks*
Homi K. Bhabha's *The Location of Culture*
Gustavo Gutiérrez's *A Theology of Liberation*
Edward Said's *Orientalism*
Gayatri Chakravorty Spivak's *Can the Subaltern Speak?*

PSYCHOLOGY

Gordon Allport's *The Nature of Prejudice*
Alan Baddeley & Graham Hitch's *Aggression: A Social Learning Analysis*
Albert Bandura's *Aggression: A Social Learning Analysis*
Leon Festinger's *A Theory of Cognitive Dissonance*
Sigmund Freud's *The Interpretation of Dreams*
Betty Friedan's *The Feminine Mystique*
Michael R. Gottfredson & Travis Hirschi's *A General Theory of Crime*
Eric Hoffer's *The True Believer: Thoughts on the Nature of Mass Movements*
William James's *Principles of Psychology*
Elizabeth Loftus's *Eyewitness Testimony*
A. H. Maslow's *A Theory of Human Motivation*
Stanley Milgram's *Obedience to Authority*
Steven Pinker's *The Better Angels of Our Nature*
Oliver Sacks's *The Man Who Mistook His Wife For a Hat*
Richard Thaler & Cass Sunstein's *Nudge: Improving Decisions About Health, Wealth and Happiness*
Amos Tversky's *Judgment under Uncertainty: Heuristics and Biases*
Philip Zimbardo's *The Lucifer Effect*

SCIENCE

Rachel Carson's *Silent Spring*
William Cronon's *Nature's Metropolis: Chicago And The Great West*
Alfred W. Crosby's *The Columbian Exchange*
Charles Darwin's *On the Origin of Species*
Richard Dawkin's *The Selfish Gene*
Thomas Kuhn's *The Structure of Scientific Revolutions*
Geoffrey Parker's *Global Crisis: War, Climate Change and Catastrophe in the Seventeenth Century*
Mathis Wackernagel & William Rees's *Our Ecological Footprint*

SOCIOLOGY

Michelle Alexander's *The New Jim Crow: Mass Incarceration in the Age of Colorblindness*
Gordon Allport's *The Nature of Prejudice*
Albert Bandura's *Aggression: A Social Learning Analysis*
Hanna Batatu's *The Old Social Classes And The Revolutionary Movements Of Iraq*
Ha-Joon Chang's *Kicking Away the Ladder*
W. E. B. Du Bois's *The Souls of Black Folk*
Émile Durkheim's *On Suicide*
Frantz Fanon's *Black Skin, White Masks*
Frantz Fanon's *The Wretched of the Earth*
Eric Foner's *Reconstruction: America's Unfinished Revolution, 1863-1877*
Eugene Genovese's *Roll, Jordan, Roll: The World the Slaves Made*
Jack Goldstone's *Revolution and Rebellion in the Early Modern World*
Antonio Gramsci's *The Prison Notebooks*
Richard Herrnstein & Charles A Murray's *The Bell Curve: Intelligence and Class Structure in American Life*
Eric Hoffer's *The True Believer: Thoughts on the Nature of Mass Movements*
Jane Jacobs's *The Death and Life of Great American Cities*
Robert Lucas's *Why Doesn't Capital Flow from Rich to Poor Countries?*
Jay Macleod's *Ain't No Makin' It: Aspirations and Attainment in a Low Income Neighborhood*
Elaine May's *Homeward Bound: American Families in the Cold War Era*
Douglas McGregor's *The Human Side of Enterprise*
C. Wright Mills's *The Sociological Imagination*

Macat Disciplines

Access the greatest ideas and thinkers across entire disciplines, including

INEQUALITY

Ha-Joon Chang's, *Kicking Away the Ladder*

David Graeber's, *Debt: The First 5000 Years*

Robert E. Lucas's, *Why Doesn't Capital Flow from Rich To Poor Countries?*

Thomas Piketty's, *Capital in the Twenty-First Century*

Amartya Sen's, *Inequality Re-Examined*

Mahbub Ul Haq's, *Reflections on Human Development*

Macat analyses are available from all good bookshops and libraries.

Access hundreds of analyses through one, multimedia tool.

Join free for one month **library.macat.com**

Macat Disciplines

Access the greatest ideas and thinkers across entire disciplines, including

CRIMINOLOGY

Michelle Alexander's
The New Jim Crow: Mass Incarceration in the Age of Colorblindness

Michael R. Gottfredson & Travis Hirschi's
A General Theory of Crime

Elizabeth Loftus's
Eyewitness Testimony

Richard Herrnstein & Charles A. Murray's
The Bell Curve: Intelligence and Class Structure in American Life

Jay Macleod's
Ain't No Makin' It: Aspirations and Attainment in a Low-Income Neighborhood

Philip Zimbardo's
The Lucifer Effect

Macat Disciplines

Access the greatest ideas and thinkers across entire disciplines, including

GLOBALIZATION

Arjun Appadurai's, *Modernity at Large: Cultural Dimensions of Globalisation*

James Ferguson's, *The Anti-Politics Machine*

Geert Hofstede's, *Culture's Consequences*

Amartya Sen's, *Development as Freedom*

Macat Disciplines

Access the greatest ideas and thinkers across entire disciplines, including

MAN AND THE ENVIRONMENT

 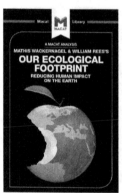

The Brundtland Report's, *Our Common Future*
Rachel Carson's, *Silent Spring*
James Lovelock's, *Gaia: A New Look at Life on Earth*
Mathis Wackernagel & William Rees's, *Our Ecological Footprint*

Macat analyses are available from all good bookshops and libraries.

Access hundreds of analyses through one, multimedia tool.
Join free for one month **library.macat.com**

Macat Disciplines

Access the greatest ideas and thinkers across entire disciplines, including

THE FUTURE OF DEMOCRACY

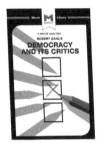

Robert A. Dahl's, *Democracy and Its Critics*
Robert A. Dahl's, *Who Governs?*
Alexis De Toqueville's, *Democracy in America*
Niccolò Machiavelli's, *The Prince*
John Stuart Mill's, *On Liberty*
Robert D. Putnam's, *Bowling Alone*
Jean-Jacques Rousseau's, *The Social Contract*
Henry David Thoreau's, *Civil Disobedience*

Printed in the United States
by Baker & Taylor Publisher Services